THE COLERIDGE WAY COMPANION GUIDE
Second Edition

IAN PEARSON

GW00645265

Published by Ian Pearson
The Old Cider House, 25 Castle Street,
Nether Stowey, Somerset TA5 1LN

ISBN 978-0-9933573-1-2

For more details and updates:
www.coleridgewaywalk.co.uk

All photographs © Ian Pearson

Front cover: Ian Pearson and Ian Faris outside Coleridge Cottage
Back cover, Ozy the Labrador | Plaque at Coleridge Cottage

With thanks to:

Lynne
Glennys
Alan

and

Ozy the Labrador

CONTENTS

BEST LAID PLANS – AN INTRODUCTION

In November 2013 I approached the Coleridge Way Steering Committee with a plan to write a travel guide for the soon to be extended Coleridge Way. The Committee gave the nod and for the next five months I planned, scribbled, researched, trained, interviewed and generally psyched myself up for the 51 mile walk starting at the beginning of June 2014.

In the third week of May I was in hospital having the six deconstructed pieces of my left arm pinned, plated and wired back together after a bit of a topple off a bicycle. This was, I have to say, a bit of a setback.

My surgeon said there was no way that I would be able to walk the route and, to a certain extent, he was correct. However, he didn't tell me that I couldn't hitch, limp and bus the route and that's exactly what I did. I spent a lot of time researching in local pubs, talking to locals about what the path meant to them and garnering sympathy and admiration for undertaking the walk with one arm in plaster (I tended to gloss over the fact that I'd not actually walked that day).

Within a month, I was back to somewhere near full fitness, or at least the level of fitness expected of a fifty year old, one armed, food loving, brewer, and the walk commenced once again.

It was my original intention to loop the walk back to Nether Stowey via the Devon and Somerset coast paths. However, at the time this was impossible as sections of coast path just did not exist. This difficulty resolved itself with the opening of the England Coast Path in March 2016 which allowed walkers to walk 58 miles from Brean Down to Minehead for the first time.

This book is therefore a combination of three separate weeks in the life of the Coleridge Way and a further two journeys along the coast paths. On all of these walks I was accompanied by Ozy, my now fourteen year old black Labrador who kept me sane, or at least allowed me to talk to myself without appearing too mad.

Along the way Ozy and I bumped into loads of interesting people and those people provided me with a cornucopia of interesting facts and stories about the area, the path and the people along it.

So, the Coleridge Way – what exactly is it?

Well, at its most basic level it's a 51 mile, mid-distance walking trail from the Quantock village of Nether Stowey in the east to the seaside town of Lynmouth in Exmoor, Devon. It started life in 2005 as a slightly shorter 36 mile route, ending at Porlock and I had the honour of being the first person to walk it then. The path was extended in May 2014 to include

locations relevant to Samuel Taylor Coleridge's stay in the area; including Culbone where Coleridge wrote (and forgot a lot of) Kubla Khan and the Valley of the Rocks just past Lynmouth.

Once at Lynmouth, the new England Coast Path joins up the South West Coast Path and the West Somerset Coastal Path and eventually back to Nether Stowey via the new Two Castles' Way. This makes the route a total of a hundred miles through some of the most beautiful, unspoiled, and unknown areas of the UK. A perfect week's walk.

The Coleridge Way takes its walkers through picturesque countryside, deep and challenging combes, ancient woodlands, heather capped moors and spectacular coastal paths, all of which come with stunning views over the Bristol Channel into Wales.

The route is billed as 'a walk in the footsteps of the romantic poets', in the plural, as not only Coleridge walked these paths and tracks, but his friends William and Dorothy Wordsworth joined him for a year at the end of the eighteenth century.

The reality of the situation is slightly more prosaic in that the path was conceived as a boost to the rural economy after the devastating effects of foot and mouth disease in 2001. The government, both national and local, needed to bring people back into the countryside and for Exmoor and the

Quantocks, what better way than a mid-distance path over some of the most unexplored countryside in the UK?

At fifty-odd miles the Coleridge Way itself is an ideal long weekend's break with plenty of accommodation, pubs and shops along the way. I walked the path to Lynmouth over three, four and five days and the return trip over four, although the coastal route is easier and I could have easily walked this over three days.

This book is designed to be a standalone travelogue, a gazetteer of interesting facts and a basic route-guide to enable the reader to get the best out of the path and would make an ideal bedtime read along the route so that walkers are prepared for the next day's hiking.

Whilst this guide helps walkers to enjoy the route, they will also need to download the most up-to-date route directions from www.coleridgeway.co.uk and should also consider buying the two Ordnance Survey maps covering the path; Explorer 140 Quantock Hills and Bridgwater and Explorer OL9 Exmoor or the Yellow Zigzag guide.

Further information is available from www.coleridgewaywalk.co.uk and a Twitter feed - @coleridgeway has up to date information about the route. Walkers are encouraged to send anything relevant to that Twitter account using the hashtag #coleridgeway. Photos, anecdotes or route notes/corrections are all gratefully received.

Just a quick note about distances in this guide. The basic directions contain the distance from one point to another. These are very much an estimation with yards and metres being interchangeable. A hundred yards is a couple of minutes' walk, 400 yards and a ¼ mile are about 5-10 minutes' walk, half a mile 10-20 minutes' walk and a mile 20-30 minutes' walk. However, these distances should be obvious. Anything described as 'a good' something (e.g. "a good mile") means that the timing will be at the top limit. Where the path is obvious, the directions are less detailed and where the path gets difficult a more detailed explanation is provided.

In May 2007 The Coleridge Bridle Way was launched for horse and rider. This follows a slightly different route, although most of the information in this book is relevant to riders as well as walkers.

In addition, I took along a voice recorder with me and pointed a microphone at anyone willing to speak to me. These recordings have been turned into short 'audioblogs' which can be heard at www.coleridgewaywalk.co.uk.

Being that this is a literary walk, there are also a number of poems to be read along the route by way of QR codes readable by a smart-phone. QR stands for Quick Response and is a matrix barcode etched onto a square of slate and attached to signposts. Usually these codes are used to direct people to a particular website (like the one over the page) but they also contain coded text, in this case in the form of short poems. You will

need a QR reader for your phone and this can be downloaded for free quickly and easily prior to starting the walk. Just search for 'QR code reader' in your apps store. Also you do not need mobile coverage to read the poems as the codes contain all the information necessary.

There is plenty of accommodation along the route and details of these can be found on the various Coleridge Way websites. It is recommended that accommodation is booked in advance as some of the smaller villages may have limited bed spaces, especially in high season or very low season because of winter closures. For B&Bs off the route, kindly owners may give you a lift to and from your stopping off point or a private bus service, the Moor Rover (www.atwest.org.uk) can be booked.

Many of the accommodation providers allow dogs and Ozy found little difficulty finding places to stay. All but one pub along the original 51 mile route allowed dogs in their premises, but it is always polite to ask as there may be rules about which areas are accessible to our canine companions. The coastal towns had plenty of accommodation and pubs allowing dogs.

Luggage transfer services are available either from the Moor Rover (see above) or www.luggagetransfers.co.uk. Alternatively, you could try and butter up your accommodation provider to take your luggage on. Providers will usually charge £10-£15 for this service. The local taxi firms will also take luggage but charge the standard rate and this can be a bit pricey.

All but the smallest villages along the route have a pub and a shop for refreshments. Occasionally the nearest pub will be slightly off the path. If you want your accommodation provider to provide a packed lunch, order this well in advance to give them some time to buy in the essentials.

A number of the villages have a cashpoint, even if this is within the convenience store or petrol station, however, many of these make a charge for withdrawals. Some of the smaller accommodation providers will not take credit or debit cards and so remember to keep sufficient cash available for these as well as for drinks in pubs – this is not London you know!

Whilst it is possible to start the walk from either end, it makes most sense to start from Coleridge Cottage in Nether Stowey – it just feels right. The upside of doing this is that you will walk from east to west, keeping the sun out of your eyes in the morning. The downside is that the wind comes predominantly from the west. Of course, on the return trip the opposite applies.

Nether Stowey is easily accessible by car and there is a car park by the library in Castle Street. Alternatively, some of the B&Bs will let you park on their property if you are staying with them, occasionally asking for a small donation to charity.

There is a regular bus service from Bridgwater to Nether Stowey and a somewhat more limited service from Taunton, both of which have railway stations. A quick search on the Internet will give you train and bus times. A local taxi is also available when the buses are not running, including on a Sunday.

Coleridge Cottage, from where the walk starts, is owned by the National Trust and opens from March to October on all days apart from Tuesdays and Wednesdays with occasional specials around Christmas.

The Cottage won, not one, but two tourism awards in 2014; gold in the small visitor attraction category at the South West Tourism Excellence awards and silver at the national Visit England Awards for Excellence for best small visitor attraction.

Walkers tend to come down the day before the walk, visit the Cottage, stay overnight in one of the many B&Bs, ready for an early start the following day.

So with walking boots on feet and a rucksack on your back (or daysack if you are taking advantage of the luggage transfer services available in the area) join me and Ozy on a fascinating journey exploring the Coleridge Way.

Ian Pearson

COLERIDGE COTTAGE AND A SPY

It was the evening before the start of the walk and I rapped upon the brass knocker of number 37 Lime Street, Nether Stowey - better known as Coleridge Cottage. I heard the knock reverberate around the old house together with the ponderous footsteps of one of its occupants. The door swept open and a gentleman dressed in black riding boots, white pantaloons, weskit and cutaway coat with cravat and felt riding hat greeted me.

"Did you bring the needle and thread?" said the man to me and I brandished the said items.

This is Ian Faris in the guise of James Walsh, the government spy sent down from London to investigate Coleridge and Wordsworth and their nefarious republican activities. Ian had had a wardrobe malfunction requiring some deft needlework in the nether regions of his costume.

While Ian sorted himself out, plunging the needle perilously close to his unmentionables, I wandered round the downstairs of the house, silent now that the National Trust hordes had departed for the day, and got a feel for how it would have been some two hundred years ago when the Coleridges first came here at the very beginning of 1797.

The downstairs rooms are small and bare, and whilst a little gloomy, probably lighter than they were when the Coleridges lived here over two hundred years ago. Coleridge called the cottage, then named Gilbards, the 'hovel' and it was not in the best of condition.

"That's better." Ian informed me, now somewhat more correctly attired. "Shall we start our tour with the welcome parlour?"

This room recreated that first winter's night when Samuel, Sara(h) and their infant son, Hartley, arrived at their small rented property on the outskirts of the village. Trunks and boxes are stacked ready to be unpacked. The room is dark with the only light coming from the open fire containing the half burnt remains of the Watchman magazine.

Sarah Coleridge was usually referred to as Sara by her husband and the spellings are interchangeable – just to clear up any confusion.

The Watchman was published by Coleridge for three months in 1796. Interestingly it was published every eight days to avoid tax; newspapers being heavily taxed at the time to control *'hatred and contempt of the Government and holy religion'* and, in effect, pricing out the poor from reading anything that might upset the status quo.

Coleridge's publication aimed to *proclaim the State of the Political Atmosphere, and preserve Freedom and her Friends from the attacks of Robbers and Assassins!* He called it a 'miscellany', a collection of diverse topics that would appeal to a wide variety of 'right thinking' readers. However, often the articles were viewed as seditious attacks on the government and close to treason.

What it also contained were Coleridge's early poems including *'To a Young lady, with a Poem on the French Revolution'* which gave the reader some insight as to the state of Coleridge's mind and political persuasion.

Unfortunately, the magazine relied upon subscriptions and despite Coleridge's tour of the Midlands and North of England to seek out some of the more dissenting voices in the hothouses of the north the publication failed even though Coleridge suggested that it made a *'bread-and-cheesish profit'*. However, the more pressing costs of baby-linen and the funeral expenses of Sara's mother took precedence over this vanity publication.

Coleridge explains the publication's demise in his tenth and last address;

> *The reason is short and satisfactory - the Work does not pay its expenses. Part of my Subscribers have relinquished it because it did not contain sufficient original composition, and a still larger number because it contained too much'.*

However, it was the fact that the paper is actually in the hearth that excited Ian and the fact that the maid had been berated by Coleridge for using it as kindling thinking the paper of having no value (which was probably true).

This welcome parlour forms part of the original cottage built in around 1640 or 1650 and probably differs little from how it looked some 218 years ago. The cottage was smaller then than now and given the frequent visitors would have been cramped.

In May 1797 both the Wordsworths and Charles Lamb, the writer and essayist, descended on the cottage, making for a very uncomfortable time. Especially as Coleridge was laid up with scalded feet due to a boiling milk 'accident'. This incident may well have been an attempt by Sara to stop Coleridge from spending time out walking with his friends, especially Dorothy Wordsworth.

But time is pressing and Ian was keen to show me Sara's kitchen, just across the corridor.

This room was a general utility room and looks the part with gleaming copper pots and pans, tallow candles attached to the wall to stop the numerous mice and rats eating them and Coleridge's sodden undies hanging up to drip dry into a bucket.

"Do you like a curry?" asked Ian, tearing my attention away from the undies.

"Er, yes." I replied and Ian went on to explain that curries are not a recent invention and have been around for centuries.

Sara Coleridge came from Bristol and, with its docks and frequent ships arriving from the East Indies, spices would have been readily available with mid-century cookery books already having recipes for curries and pilaus. I had rather hoped that I'd be offered a taste of this ancient culinary delight; however the only food dotted around the kitchen all looked rather stale or perhaps made of plaster.

However, curries or not, the life of an eighteenth century housewife was not easy. Sara would have had to lift the heavy pans and skillets, fetch water from the well to boil on the fire, sew and mend, wash nappies and look after young Hartley and her often more demanding husband who was prone to any number of illnesses, not least attributable to his now occasionally debilitating drug habit. To add to this the Coleridges took in a high maintenance epileptic lodger, one Charles Lloyd (of the banking family), who eventually had to be placed in a sanatorium.

With no curry appearing we then made our way into the main parlour with its large open fireplace. This was probably the main living room for the family whilst they lived in Nether Stowey. The room is homely and with the fire blazing would have been warm and cosy, albeit that Sara often complained that the Lime Street property was cramped, draughty and damp – oh and smelled of sulphur.

Ian tells me that whilst Coleridge wrote most of his influential poetry whilst living in Nether Stowey, he wrote very little of it at home apart from *Frost at Midnight* which was written one cold and icy night, probably by the light of the fire or a rush candle whilst Coleridge was tending to his sleeping son, Hartley.

The poem explains to Hartley how his father was brought up in the city and that the infant's life will be so much better wandering amongst lakes and mountain crags. These descriptions are not entirely representative of the Quantocks' landscape but certainly fitted well with the family's later life in the Lake District.

On the high mantelpiece is a bottle containing tincture of opium, laudanum, Coleridge's vice. He would have used this for minor ailments, toothache and the like to start with, but soon became dependent on the drug, even making its use glamorous in certain circles.

Whilst I would have been happy to settle down in the cosy parlour, Ian soon whisked me upstairs to see where Samuel and Sara would have slept.

The small room on the right is their bedroom, simply decorated with a small bed, trunk and chest of drawers. The National Trust have tried to create that 'just hopped out of bed' look to the room and I can imagine Coleridge, in his bare feet, just popping out to empty the chamber pot.

Draped over the end of the wooden bed is a bonnet and dress, the hem of which is rather grubby. Dorothy Wordsworth, I was told, had a habit of borrowing Sara's dresses and going walking in the hills bringing them back in a dirty state and offering no apology for doing so. The women didn't get on particularly well and some have suggested that Coleridge may have been having an affair with Dorothy, although there is no evidence of this happening.

The bed had also seen more recent activity. Anecdote has it that a matter of days after the National Trust decided to give the cottage a more lived in look, and took away the ropes keeping the visitors away from the exhibits, a couple were found in the bed testing out the springs. When caught *in flagrante delicto* (so to speak) the two of them showed not an ounce of embarrassment and calmly finished off their business, readjusted their attire and left the premises.

The next room has been turned into a small museum of Coleridge memorabilia detailing his life both before and after he lived in Nether Stowey.

Portraits hang on the wall. At the age of 23 Coleridge appears youthful and full of a life well lived, yet nine years later at the age of 32, the portrait is of a man full of worry and Ian ponders upon the reasons for this. Perhaps it was because of the opium addiction, or the fact that his life had taken a very different tack. Ten years further on and Coleridge looks older than his 42 years, his dark brown locks now tinged with grey.

Coleridge was the youngest of nine children born to John and Ann Coleridge. There were also four step brothers and sisters from an earlier marriage. Young Samuel seems to have had a pleasant early childhood and was a favourite of the family, all of whom showed promise with doctors, clergy and teachers amongst them and Oxford being the preferred university. Samuel, who hated being called Samuel and preferred STC, was a bit of a child prodigy who loved reading even being caught at school reading Virgil for 'pleasure'.

However, it was the events of the time, in particular the French Revolution, that shaped the young poet's thinking and outlook on life. This continued into his university years when he went to Jesus College at Cambridge and took a toll on his studying.

Coleridge was a man whose vocabulary did not include 'frugality' and 'compromise' and his idealistic nature led him into any number of scrapes and a large amount of debt. He even bet his last funds on the Irish lottery in November 1793. This was a state controlled lottery and raised much needed funds for the Irish Government from 1780 to 1801.

The fact that Coleridge had resorted to gambling to sort out his financial difficulties prompted him to write his first published poem. The poem, *To Fortune, on Buying a Ticket in the Irish Lottery*, was published by the Morning Chronicle on 7 November 1793 and is full of despair at the impecunious situation he found himself in.

A week later Coleridge was practically suicidal and after the end of November, when it was obvious that he had not won, he took the momentous step of enlisting with the Royal Dragoons under the unlikely assumed name of Silas Tomkyn Comberbache.

Coleridge was not a born soldier, using his writing skills as currency for others tending his horse and equipment. When Samuel's brother heard of his enlistment arrangements were made for a discharge on the grounds of insanity and STC returned to Cambridge.

It was around this time that Coleridge met Robert Southey, he of *The Three Bears* fame (later becoming *Goldilocks and the Three Bears*), and they immediately became great friends with very similar political views. It was Southey who introduced his fiancée's sister, Sarah, to Coleridge, who she later married.

For the next three years Coleridge honed his political and religious ideals, met various free thinkers and radicals and published poems, gave lectures and mused.

So what brought Coleridge to Nether Stowey?

Coleridge was no stranger to the West Country having been born and brought up in Ottery St Mary in Devon. However, it was Robert Southey, who introduced him to the area in 1794. The two of them were on an expedition to Somerset and visited a fellow Cambridge student, Henry Poole, in the village of Shurton some three miles away from Nether Stowey.

Henry walked his two companions south to Nether Stowey to meet another strand of his family headed by the disagreeable and cantankerous tanner, Thomas Poole (the elder). However, it was the son, also Thomas, who struck up an immediate affinity with Coleridge.

At the time, Nether Stowey, then as now often just called 'Stowey', consisted of only three main roads; those of Lime Street and St Mary Street and at a right angle, Castle Street. If Coleridge had entered the village from the Shurton direction, via the Combwich ferry, then the first building he would have come upon would have been the house he lived in for the three years from 1797.

Poole the younger lived in Castle Street with its stream or 'stinking gutter' as Coleridge once called it, running on the south side. In fact you are not considered to be a proper Nether Stowian unless you have fallen in the brook; something that frequent visitors to any one of the three remaining hostelries occasionally do.

Tom Poole had little time for the business of the tannery, much to the chagrin of his father, and preferred reading and more intellectual pursuits. Having said this, his knowledge of the family business stood him in good stead, allowing him to be elected to speak to the Prime Minister on the issues facing a beleaguered tanning industry because of the scarcity of the sessile oak bark in the Somerset area.

When Poole and Coleridge first met, it was for just one day, however, Poole's revolutionary political ideas and religious standpoint (he was a deist believing in the existence of God from observation of the natural world) meant that they got on like a house on fire.

Coleridge, in a rejection of his former city life, wanted a more rural existence and the two men probably discussed Coleridge's aspirations to set up a pantisocracy (yes, I had to look it up as well – it means government by all, a collective democracy).

It was Coleridge and Southey's intention to set up a utopian community where all men (and women) were equal and each member would only have to work two or three hours a day, no one would have power over anyone else and you grew your own veg; a sort of eighteenth century kibbutz but without the wine and sandals.

Coleridge believed that all suffering and crime stemmed from social inequality and to alleviate this no one should privately hold property, it should belong to all.

The original planned location for this commune was destined to be located by the Susquehanna River in New England (USA). However, this location became increasingly untenable with Southey suggesting Wales as an alternative. Later Southey went off the whole idea completely, becoming a lawyer, something for which Coleridge never forgave him. With the utopian dream in tatters perhaps Nether Stowey was a better bet?

Coleridge came back to Stowey in September 1795 after Thomas Poole the elder had died and Tom Poole welcomed his friend with a poem starting, *'Hail to thee Coleridge, youth of various powers'*! Whilst this was a lovely sentiment, Coleridge was unable to stay and went back to Bristol. However, through correspondence, the two men's friendship grew stronger and this prompted a further visit in the spring of 1796 when Poole suggested supplying Coleridge with an annuity of £35 or £40, perhaps £25,000 in today's money.

It was when Coleridge was on his way back home from Nether Stowey at this time, and possibly because of the recent failure of the Watchman, that he wrote to Poole from Bridgwater to say that he had to do something with his life as *'Those two giants, yclept BREAD & CHEESE end me to compliance'*. (For those of you who have no idea what 'yclept' is – it means 'by the name of' from the Old English 'gecleopod'). The £35 or £40 wasn't however, enough to keep him in Stowey that year.

It was probably the birth of Coleridge's son that convinced him to return and to live in Nether Stowey. In the spirit of his pantisocratic vision for the world, Coleridge wanted his children to grow up in an environment *'in the simplicity of peasants, their food, dress and habits completely rustic'*. Lucky Hartley! Stowey fulfilled that desire.

After searching for a property in the area, the run-down cottage that Coleridge had first glimpsed as he entered the village some three years previously was suggested as an, albeit not perfect, short let.

However, the house fitted in with Coleridge's communalist vision of society and the garden would allow vegetables to be grown to feed the family and to give them something to work at. The house was, however, cold and Coleridge didn't relish that.

Whilst the cottage was a little miserable, Thomas Poole's house in Castle Street, which was just a short stroll away through the orchards at the back, was warm and comfortable and STC, if not Sara and Hartley, spent a great deal of time there.

I would be passing Poole House tomorrow on my walk and would take the opportunity to peer in through the window to see where Coleridge spent much of his time.

For now Ian had finished his tour. I asked him what happened to the cottage after Coleridge had left and was told that the cottage was refurbished and in the nineteenth century it was enlarged when it became Moore's Coleridge Cottage Inn.

The building was acquired by the National Trust in 1908 and its present layout, with the additional rooms upstairs, appeared in 1998.

THE ANCIENT MARINER - PUB AND POEM

At the mention of the word 'inn' Ian's eyes lit up (as did mine) and it was decided to pop into the local hostelries to continue our conversation.

Now, I have to declare an interest in the next part of the story. One of the reasons for visiting the pubs (in fact we visited all three) was that I also run Somerset's smallest commercial brewery, the Stowey Brewery, and what better place to taste these fine ales than in their home town!

Our first port of call was the Ancient Mariner, right opposite the cottage. This is a mock Tudor fronted building with its somewhat modernistic pub sign depicting the first edition of the *Lyrical Ballads*.

I had expected Ian to change out of his costume but, curiously, he seemed to feel very comfortable in it and we entered the pub with all eyes on us – well, on Ian actually.

We ordered two of the finest pints available in the county of Somersetshire and I asked Ian about James Walsh the man whose persona he had well and truly hijacked.

Ian explained that things change little over the centuries and complaints about the erosion of our liberty were just as prevalent in Coleridge's time as they are for today's whistle-blowers.

So, why was Coleridge under surveillance by Mr Walsh?

It was the time of the French Revolution, still rumbling on since 1789. The ripples from the momentous events in France had caused monarchies and theocracies to tumble around the World and in turn republics and democracies to spring up in their place. And here was Coleridge stirring up trouble.

Both Coleridge and Wordsworth had been vocal in their enthusiasm for the revolution. They had also briefly entertained Britain's Public Enemy Number One, John Thelwall, a political activist and journalist who had been tried, and acquitted, of treason. This did not, however, stop the government of the day keeping tabs on him and those that associated with him. Therefore Walsh was dispatched to deepest Somerset.

Thelwall stayed with Coleridge in Nether Stowey and Wordsworth in Alfoxton and, being tired of politics, greatly enjoyed the rural lifestyle that the two poets had adopted. Coleridge called Thelwall 'Citizen John' and suggested that the Quantocks were an ideal place to talk about treason. Thelwall's response was that this was 'a fine place to make man forget that there is any necessity for treason'. However, even Coleridge was aware of the political dangers of hanging around with Thelwall and put him off settling down in the area.

Actually, I prefer the somewhat more amusing story of why Walsh was here.

When the Wordsworths moved into Alfoxton (more of this later), they were provided with a houseman. However, given the poet and his sister's thick Lakeland accents, the houseman couldn't understand a word they were saying and thought they were speaking French, (or Spanish or Dutch - they were all expected to invade at any moment). This together with their long, night-time rambles, no doubt to signal to passing ships, caused him to report them to the authorities.

It appears that Walsh either wasn't particularly good at hiding his presence, or didn't care, but Coleridge was well aware of his presence and called him 'Spy Nozy.' Whatever, Walsh ultimately decided that the poets were of no threat to national security and scuttled back to civilized London.

Oh that beer was good.

The Ancient Mariner was originally called The First and Last, being both the first and last pub in the village. Its age is not known precisely, but first mention of it appears in 1871 and the name was changed to the current one in 1982. However, its relatively young age didn't deter a couple of American tourists who were overheard to say (cue bad Mid-West accent); "Well, this must have been where Coleridge got the idea for his poem"!

So, where did Coleridge get the idea?

It was always thought that the idea came to Coleridge while he was out walking with William Wordsworth in the Quantock Hills. Wordsworth recounted the story later, explaining that he and Coleridge had talked together about a book by Captain George Shelvocke, *A Voyage round the World by Way of the Great South Sea,* published in 1726. In the book, a miserable sailor shoots a black albatross.

In addition, this story may have been enhanced by the watery, sunlit mist that envelopes the northern Levels and silty Parrett estuary with its mud fishermen plying their trade. Coleridge would have witnessed these ghostlike figures just a few miles from Nether Stowey and at least one fisherman still carries on this ancient and nearly forgotten craft.

In the shadow of Hinkley Point power station Brendan Sellick from the tiny coastal village of Stolford is the fourth generation of his family to fish the estuary using a 'mud horse' harvesting brown shrimps, elvers and even bass, sole and cod.

The mud horse looks like a single wooden sleigh with a large surface area blade stopping the contraption and its rider from sinking into the mud. These contraptions have been used in the area for over 4,000 years and are a highly efficient method of travelling over even the sloppiest of mud and silt.

The Rime of the Ancyent Marinere was written in 1797 or 98 and appeared in the first edition of the *Lyrical Ballads (with a Few Other Poems).* This collection of poems is generally accepted to have marked the beginning of the English Romantic movement in literature. It was a collaboration with William Wordsworth who wrote most of the poems. However, it was the Ancient Mariner that caught the readers' imaginations and propelled Coleridge into greatness.

The Lyrical Ballads were an attempt to overturn the very structured and intellectual style of poetry that had been fashionable in the eighteenth century and hoped to bring poetry to the masses, using every-day and understandable language. One writer has suggested that this was poetry entering its 'punk' stage and it also followed on from the French Revolution and the 'power to the people' mandate that both poets subscribed to.

The Rime of the Ancient Mariner is certainly Coleridge's longest major poem and tells the story of a sailor who stops an unsuspecting wedding guest to tell him the tale of his life. The wedding guest is at first annoyed at being waylaid, but soon becomes engrossed in the story with its tragic consequences. The poem is a cross between the story of the Wandering Jew and the Flying Dutchman.

For those who don't know the poem it goes something like this...

A ship starts a journey but is blown off course eventually reaching Antarctica. An albatross appears and guides the ship back on course. However, the Mariner shoots the bird which initially brings criticism from the crew but later praise as the weather becomes warmer. This state of affairs doesn't last as the ship enters unchartered waters and is becalmed.

Day after day, day after day,
We stuck, nor breath nor motion;
As idle as a painted ship
Upon a painted ocean.

The fickle sailors revert to blaming the Mariner for their situation and lack of drinking water,

Water, water, everywhere,
And all the boards did shrink;
Water, water, everywhere,
Nor any drop to drink.

and force him to wear the albatross around his neck as a penance.

A ghostly vessel appears with 'Death' and 'Nightmare Life in Death' playing dice for the lives of the crew and the Mariner. Death wins the crew, Life in Death the Mariner.

All the crew die but the Mariner lives on with the corpses of his former crewmates.

The curse is finally lifted after he understands God's goodness and manages to pray. The albatross falls off and the crew come back to life and steer the ship back home only to be swallowed up by a whirlpool.

The Mariner is rescued and rows ashore and as a penance is forced to wander the earth and tell his story. All good stuff.

A statue of the Mariner stands on Watchet Harbour and given Watchet's proximity to the path, perhaps it would have been a worthy detour for the route.

The tale of the Ancient Mariner is enduring, even though the story, albeit somewhat convoluted, doesn't really have a moral and doesn't really go anywhere! However, plenty of modern artistes have used the poem, often in pop songs including; Iron Maiden (*the Rime of the Ancient Mariner*), Pink Floyd (*Echoes*) and Fleetwood Mac (*Albatross*).

Oh, and of course the albatross around the neck is now a metaphor for a psychological burden that someone has to carry. Interestingly, Coleridge coined (or influenced) a number of other phrases that have entered common parlance including; 'Achilles' heel', 'pipe dream' and 'suspension of disbelief'.

Whilst a second pint beckoned, there were two other pubs to visit and Ian and I headed into the centre of the village to the next, the George Hotel.

This hostelry is reputed to be the oldest existing pub in the village with references going back to 1616. However this is unlikely to have been the original site of the pub with the first George being on the opposite side of the street with a bowling green and 'fives' wall. This had closed by 1781 and was rebuilt in 1843 as a private house. The current pub was built or converted by 1804, but with its bare stone walls and cosy atmosphere it felt like it had been there forever.

Ian and I were greeted by Bill, the present landlord, and the soft strains of northern soul being played over the PA system. No Stowey Ale here, but being of a magnanimous nature we drank the local Exmoor Ale. Ian still attracted sidelong glances from the pub's customers, but all were far too polite to mention his attire.

The George is a bit of an enigma with little of its history surviving although British History On-line states that in 1899 and 1906 it had assembly rooms where 'theatrical entertainments' were given.

Opposite the George is the Old Gaol and in the early 1870's this accommodated a tame dancing bear. It appears that a traveller was passing through the village but could find no accommodation willing to put him and the bear up. I'm sure the George would now – it's very pet friendly!

It was also here that the wife of a man detained in the lock-up, which was then enclosed, fed him beer through a long clay pipe, pushing the thin end of the stem through the keyhole and inserting the other end into a tankard of ale.

Our last port of call is the pub next door, the Rose and Crown.

References to this pub post-date the George, but not having moved, this is probably the oldest surviving drinking establishment in the village.

The bar area is bare wood and stone floored with photos of the village adorning the walls. We were greeted by the landlord Charles who, being used to seeing Ian in his garb, again makes no comment.

It was here that Tom Poole's friendly society for working women was founded in 1807 and continued up until the 1970s. This philanthropic movement is still commemorated each year with the Women's Walk in late June, where the women of the village meet to parade to St Mary's Church to the strains of a brass band.

Whilst the Rose and Crown now offers comfortable en-suite accommodation, this has not always been the case.

In 1618 the eccentric poet and traveller, John Taylor, visited the village. Taylor started life as a Thames boatman and waterman and also served in the Navy. He became famous for a series of whimsical journeys; including sailing from London to Queenborough, Kent, in a paper boat with two stockfish tied to canes for oars and a trip he made on foot from London to Edinburgh without any money.

Taylor started his Quantock adventure at Bridgwater where he managed to tear his breeches and had to debag and find a *'botching threepenny tailor'* to patch them up for him. He then trotted 'five miles further to a ragged market town called Neatherstoy.' where he took up lodgings at the Rose and Crown where the *'Roses are withered, and Crowns are obscured, as the sign was.'*.

I'll let Mr Taylor describe the experience in his own words…

Surely that day was a mad, sad, glad, auspicious, unlucky day to me, worse than an ominous, childermas or a dogged biting dog-day; for the hostess was out of town, mine host was very sufficiently drunk, the house most delicately decked with exquisite artificial, and natural sluttery, the room besprinkled and strewed with the excrements of pigs and children:

the wall and ceilings were adorned and hanged with rare spider's tapestry, or cobweb-lawn; the smoke was so palpable and perspicuous, that I could scarce see anything else, and yet I could scarce see that, it so blinded me with rheum a sign of weeping; besides all this, the odourous and contagious perfume of that house was able to outvie all the milliners in Christendom or Somersetshire.

I being thus embellished, or encompassed with these most unmatchable varieties, but to comfort me completely, mine host swigged off half a pot to me, bade me be merry, and asked me if I would have any powdered beef and carrots to supper. I told him yes, with all my heart... I went into the house to see if supper were ready; but I found small comfort there, for the fire was out, no beef to be boiled, mine host fast asleep, the maid attending the hogs, and my hungry self half-starved with expectation.

I awaked mine host, and asked him where the beef was, he told me that he had none, and desired me to be contented with eggs fried with parsley. I prayed him to show me my chamber, which he did. The chamber was suitable to the rest of the house, there I staid till near nine o'clock, expecting fried eggs, when mine host came to me with an empty answer, there were no eggs to be had, so at the last I purchased a piece of bread and butter, and to bed, and then began my further torments.

I was furiously assaulted by an Ethiopian army of fleas, and do verily believe that I laid so manfully about me that I made more than 500 mortuus est : they were so well grown that as I took 'em I gave 'em no quarter, but rubbed 'em between my finger and my thumb, and they were so plump and mellow, that they would squash to pieces like young boiled peas.

For my further delight, my chamber-pot seemed to be lined within with crimson plush, or shagged scarlet baize, it had 'scaped a scouring time out of mind, it was furred with antiquity, and withal it had a monumental savour, and this piss-pot was another of my best contentments.

And we all thought that Trip Advisor was a new phenomenon!

20

The Rose and Crown, Nether Stowey

"Room besprinkled with excrement of pigs and children"
⊙OOOO Reviewed 28 December 1618

Disliked - Everything   **Liked** - Leaving

⊙OOOO Value   ⊙OOOO Rooms
⊙OOOO Location   ⊙OOOO Cleanliness
⊙OOOO Check-in   ⊙OOOO Service
⊙OOOO Sleep quality

Senior reviewer – 100s of helpful votes

It is a shame that some of the other pubs are no longer in existence. The Swan, renamed the Globe (1647 – 1850), in St Mary's Street served as the local magistrates court and mortuary, The Globe in Castle Street was the place for gypsies and underage drinking and is still remembered with some fondness by older members of the village, The Bakers Arms, also in Castle Street and The Three Mariners – they would have made a fantastic pub crawl!

But our evening's drinking was over as Ian and I wobbled out of the Rose and Crown studiously avoiding falling in the brook and becoming a true Nether Stowian before I wished Ian a good night.

As I walked up Castle Street alone I could picture STC doing the same, avoiding the same brook, thinking about bread and cheese for supper and planning his next day's walk into the Quantock Hills.

For tomorrow I set out in the footsteps of this great man…

NETHER STOWEY AND RUM FOR BREAKFAST

If you are setting out in the footsteps of one of our greatest poets, then you should breakfast like one; and Coleridge may well have started the day with a steaming bowl of furmity.

Furmity (or possibly frumenty) is an oat and dried fruit porridge or gruel which was popular all around Europe from medieval times and it has been said that it is England's oldest national dish. The steaming bowl in front of me contained cream, soft brown sugar and a generous slosh of dark rum and every spoonful gave me the enthusiasm to stride out into the day. I just hoped that I don't have a hangover before elevenses.

Furmity has also found its way into English literature with the snapdragon flies living off it in Lewis Carroll's *Through the Looking-Glass*. But it is in *The Mayor of Casterbridge* by Thomas Hardy that it gets star billing and the reason the Mayor sold his wife at the beginning of the novel. So, what's the connection between Hardy's novel and the Coleridge Way? Well, the fictional Henchard (the Mayor), may well be based on an actual individual who lived just a few miles from where I now sat.

In the novel, Henchard, a young hay-trusser overindulges in the furmity tent at the local fair and, under the influence of far too much liquor, argues with his wife, Susan and sells her and their daughter at auction for five guineas to a passing sailor.

In the Quantock version, an eighteenth century agricultural labourer by the name of Bodger sold his wife, Betty, at the Bridgwater Fair (which still occurs today – the fair, not the wife selling!) as she failed to bear him

> Furmity Recipe (serves 2):
>
> 1 cup jumbo oats
> 2 cups whole milk
> 1/4 cup sultanas
> Pinch of salt
>
> Cook porridge in normal way, slowly over low heat.
>
> At end of cooking add:
>
> Light brown sugar to taste
> Good slug of dark rum
> 1/4 cup double cream.

any children. This story has a somewhat more positive ending with Betty living happily ever after, producing numerous children with her new husband. It is not known what happened to Bodger, although there is no record of him becoming mayor.

So there I was, consuming furmity and Ozy the Labrador was eating kibble. Ozy has eaten kibble for every breakfast for the last eleven years. He never tires of it and eats it with as much gusto as he did when he was a puppy. It is also his kibble and personal items that make up most of the weight and space in my rucksack. Ozy doesn't care; he has a collar and lead. All the rest is being carried by muggins here including; 1.2 kilos of food, a kilo of water, bowl, blanket, towel, chews and biscuits.

I once tried Ozy with his own rucksack. This worked perfectly until he saw a river and dived in! Since then, I've carried all his stuff for him. So fifty percent of the weight on my back belongs to Ozy. The only consolation is that this will diminish as we walk along the trail.

I've also packed four days' worth of lunches, the sort of food that Coleridge would have recognised; cheese from the local creamery, Cricketer Farm, home-made and smoked garlic, paprika and red wine sausages (carefully wrapped in eighteenth century cling film), home-baked bread using Dunster Mill wholemeal flour and to finish off my period packed lunches I had included four bars of eighteenth century Cadbury's Dairy Milk.

I was also somewhat disturbed by the headline in the West Somerset Free Press which I read over breakfast with its front page headline - 'Vets Issue Adder Alert'. It appears that Susie, a three year old Jack Russell, was bitten by an adder, the owner noticing the problem when Susie wouldn't eat a biscuit (always a sure sign of something wrong). However, all turned out right after a few hours in the vets. I therefore warned Ozy to take care and not put his nose too close to any snakes we came across.

One last thing I did before I left the house, apart from downloading a QR reader onto my phone, was to visit Chris Jelley's website, www.jelley.info and to find his 'fly catchers' page on the Coleridge Way tab.

Chris specialises in producing interactive poetry and arts projects and is the man behind the QR code poetry. His fly catcher project comes from Coleridge himself who used to call his notebooks 'fly catchers'; the method by which he snatched ideas before they flittered away. My phone now showed that I was 425 metres away from the first of these. I couldn't wait to see what would be revealed.

So with a stomach full of oats and rum (and Ozy's full of kibble) the two of us made our way back to the start of the walk at Coleridge Cottage. This involved retracing our steps from The Old Cider House to the Cottage but when starting a long-distance path, it's the event of starting that is important and to miss out on the first few hundred yards would be such a disappointment.

Ozy and I were not expecting a large send-off and we were not disappointed - we even had to take our own photograph of the start of this momentous event. But here we were, the weather looked as if it would be kind to us and we took the first step.

Behind me was the road out of the village. This would have been countryside in Coleridge's day and may possibly have been the route that Coleridge took when he first visited Stowey.

Ozy and I then walked into the centre of the village along Lime Street (the old Bridgwater to Watchet turnpike road) passing the Old Smithy with its anvil set into the wall above the door and houses that, in days gone by, had large openings for carts and carriages. Today they are all residential properties. However, of particular interest is the Quantock Savings Bank 1817 which had agents in neighbouring villages and, whilst being taken over by a national bank in later years, was another example of Thomas Poole's extraordinary philanthropic activities in the village.

Up until the 1960s this would have been the main A39 through the village and looking at the number of cars lining the left hand side of the road it would have been a nightmare to travel along until the bypass was built. The only issue now is that most travellers today completely miss the village, which is a shame.

The turnpike road ends about 150 yards further ahead joining up with the Bridgwater Turnpike which terminated at the Piper's Inn in Ashcott some 15 miles away. This part of the turnpike was used by John McAdam (Mr Tarmac) to show off his roadmaking skills.

And so to the centre of Nether Stowey.

Stowey means 'stone way' or 'paved road' and was part of the Anglo-Saxon 'Herepath', a Saxon military road starting over the other side of the River Parrett and coming through Combwich and Cannington. From here the path travels through Over Stowey and into the Quantocks.

The 'Nether' part of the name refers to the fact that it was the lower of two paths, as in the expression 'nether regions'. Over Stowey was, of course, the higher path.

We now stood where the old medieval village high cross and market house had been, known simply as the 'Cross'. The building here is now the post office and tea rooms. The circle on the wall has caused much speculation and is often thought to be a 'fire mark', the symbol to let a local private fire brigade know whether or not to put out a fire and whether the property was insured. Unfortunately, the circle's history is somewhat more mundane and it was the outer part of a sign informing National Union of Cyclists' members that they were welcome at the premises, which was then a temperance hotel.

The original market place was an octagonal open building, similar to the one in Dunster and was demolished in 1862 due to poor upkeep. However, in its time it would have dominated the scene with its quadrilateral clock and bell on the roof.

The clock had been donated by Sir Humphry Davy, who was a regular visitor to the village, again a friend of Thomas Poole, but primarily he had come to see Coleridge.

Davy was what some have described as a 'romantic chemist'; all this at a time when science and the creative arts blurred into one and intellectuals dabbled in a number of different genres. Davy was an amateur poet and Coleridge wished to 'attack chemistry, like a shark'. Davy even invited his friend to lecture on poetry at the Royal Institution in 1808. However, the difference between the two was evident. One was an incredibly driven chemist (he discovered sodium and potassium) the other a genius with a significant drug problem and countless physical ailments.

The two men had one vice in common and that was the delight in the new social fad of inhaling nitrous oxide – laughing gas. In Davy's clinical words the effect was a 'vibrant burst of pleasure', with objects becoming brighter and clearer and space seeming to expand and take on unfamiliar dimensions. A good 'trip' indeed. Coleridge was somewhat more circumspect, but poetical in describing the feeling as being 'that which I remember once to have experienced after returning from the snow into a warm room'.

The site of the market also saw more sinister activities. With rebels from the Monmouth Rebellion being hanged, drawn and quartered at the spot in 1685.

The Monmouth Rebellion was the last battle on English soil and was an attempt to overthrow the Roman Catholic, James II. The Duke of Monmouth was the illegitimate son of Charles II and claimed to be the rightful heir.

The Duke had a degree of support in the South West and hoped to raise an army of supportive troops. However, the rebellion was not to be and Monmouth's army was defeated at the Battle of Sedgemoor on 6th July 1685 with Monmouth being tried by 'Hanging' Judge Jeffreys in the Bloody Assizes.

Three Stowey men, Humphrey Mitchel, Richard Cullverell and Thomas Merrick, were arrested and were subject to the following notice of punishment by Jeffreys:

Whereas I have received a warrant under the hand and seal of the Right Honourable the Lord Jeffreys for the executing of several Rebels within your said city or village, these are therefore to will and require you immediately on sight hereof to erect a gallows in the most public place of your said city or village to hang the said Traitors on, and that you provide halters to hang them with, a sufficient number of faggots to burn the bowels of the said Traitors, and a furnace or cauldron to boil their heads and quarters, and salt to boil therewith, half a bushel to each Traitor, and tar to tar them with, and a sufficient number of spears and polls to fix and place their heads and quarters, and that you warn the owners of four oxen, at the time hereafter mentioned for execution and you yourselves together with a guard of 40 men at the least, to be present on the morning, by eight of the clock, to be aiding and assisting to me or my deputy, to see the said Rebels executed... You are also to provide an axe and a cleaver for quartering of the said Rebels.

The axe and cleaver appear to be a bit of an afterthought, but necessary all the same!

The village gaol opposite now forms part of the Jubilee Clock Tower built to commemorate Queen Victoria's long reign. Fortunately, the gaol is no longer used to hold drunks or bears but does contain information about the village and a number of Chris Jelley's QR poetry codes.

I then moved on from 'correction corner' turning right up Castle Street, soon reaching Poole House. Coleridge spent a lot of his time here and I'd arranged to have a snoop around with the current owners, Rick and Teresa.

Tom Poole was born in 1765, the eldest son of a tanner. Poole really wanted to go to university but his overbearing father denied him this opportunity; a "your grandfather was a tanner, your great-grandfather was a tanner" mentality. However, on his father's death young Thomas was able to carve his own way in the world.

While Poole never went on to higher education it did not stop him learning, for which he had a voracious appetite. He also collected an impressive library which was commented upon by the likes of William Hazlitt and Charles Lamb.

Poole was a man of the people, 'without vanity' and this made him popular with most within the village. However, he was a radical, and it was this side of him that attracted Coleridge and his friends, including Humphry Davy, William Wordsworth, the Wedgwood brothers and Andrew Crosse the mad scientist of whom we will hear more later.

Poole's philanthropic activities didn't stop at Coleridge, for whom he provided a £40 annuity, advancing money for the periodical The Friend, and supporting Hartley at Oxford. Poole also benefited many within the village including financing an elementary free school, only the second in England, (now the library) further up Castle Street. In addition he supported the Sunday school movement, formed the Stowey Female Friendly Society, and set up the village savings bank.

Every year, on the nearest Saturday to the longest day, the women of the village take part in the Women's Walk to celebrate the memory of this great man, passing by the Rose and Crown where the Women's Society used to meet and pay their weekly subscriptions to help them out in times of illness or childbirth.

After hearing so much about this unique individual I was intrigued to see inside the house.

After 200 years the house had changed, rooms had been altered, divided and enlarged but many of the features that Coleridge would have recognised were still there.

My guided tour started with the downstairs areas, a warren of rooms befitting one of the grandest buildings in the village and still retaining a little of the Georgian feel with its symmetrical sash windows, large fireplaces and differing heights in floors and ceilings.

The house has seen many uses over the years including being a shop and hairdressers. However, what I really wanted to see were those rooms and places that Coleridge would have recognised and Rick took me first into the garden and to the cypress tree at the end of the lawn. Whilst there was no evidence of a gate, this would have been where Coleridge entered the property from his cottage, no more than a hundred yards away, on his frequent trips to the house.

Our next stop was the 'Barrel Room' so called because of its barrel-vaulted ceiling and it was here that Coleridge and Wordsworth would have, read, written and, no doubt, debated ideologies with a passion.

Poole may never have known what a great influence he had had on late eighteenth century literary history by bringing together such great minds and, with this thought in my head, I bade farewell to my kind hosts, picked up Ozy and continued on my way.

Diagonally opposite and now on my left as I walked up the street are the village's oldest buildings, being medieval. Looking at the windows I can see the local double glazing firm being involved in some expensive litigation!

I passed Poole's school and Poole's tannery entrance, where some say they have seen the ghostly sight of a woman seeking her lost child who tragically drowned in the tannery millpond. Just up from here my eye was drawn to a colourful statue of a Tudor woman hidden in a nook of a wall together with her Dalmatian dog. This is Jane Seymour the wife of Henry VIII who lived near Bridgwater. Whilst the statue looks as if it has been there forever, it is a chicken wire and papier-mâché affair.

As I started to climb Castle Hill, I noted that the pink house on the left, opposite Butchers Lane, was called Christabel, another of STC's poems.

Christabel is a two part poem which Coleridge intended to be longer, but was never finished. It was planned to be part of the pre-1800 edition of the Lyrical Ballads but Wordsworth convinced Coleridge to leave it out and this may well have made Coleridge think that his days as a poet were declining.

The story is about Christabel who, on visiting woods to pray, meets Geraldine who had been abducted by some warriors.

Mary mother, save me now!
(Said Christabel) And who art thou?
...
My sire is of a noble line,
And my name is Geraldine

Christabel takes Geraldine home and then spends the night with her.

So to my room we'll creep in stealth,
And you to-night must sleep with me.

There is some disrobing and Geraldine shows Christabel a mark or wound of some description upon her breast.

Her gentle limbs did she undress,
And lay down in her loveliness.

and

Her silken robe, and inner vest,
Dropt to her feet, and full in view,
Behold! her bosom and half her side,
A sight to dream of, not to tell!

The poem is set in a Coleridgesque (I've probably invented a new word) surreal world and it has a demonic, defilement of innocence message. Modern writers also identify the sapphic elements of the work with Christabel beguiled by the beauty of the naked Geraldine. However, as the poem was never finished we shall never know quite where it was going.

At the top of Castle Hill and to the right are the remains of Nether Stowey Castle and Ozy and I took our first detour of the day to climb up to the top of its steep sided motte.

All that remain are the footings, but the outline of the castle can be clearly seen and it is well worth a visit, if only to get a first glimpse of the Quantocks and the route we would be taking into the hills.

At the top, the foundations of the castle footprint, where the family would have lived, are clearly defined. Below us are two baileys where the administration buildings stood (kitchen, brewhouse, stables etc.) together with the Church of St. Michaels.

The castle was Norman, built by Alfred d'Espaignes (not as in 'Spain' but an area in Normandy between Caen and Le Havre). Originally, Alfred may have built his HQ in Over Stowey but by late in the eleventh century had set up a permanent base here.

The castle went through a number of owners in the next couple of hundred years ending up in the Audley family in the fifteenth century.

Dr. Stuart Prior, Nether Stowey's 'Professor Castle', thinks the castle fell into general disuse in the fourteenth century having outlived its usefulness, however, I prefer the tale of beheadings, and pretenders to the throne and the tax riots that were the Perkin Warbeck Rebellion.

We all know the Princes in the Tower story, and Perkin Warbeck was supposedly one of these princes – the one that escaped, or perhaps was never incarcerated at all!

The story goes that when Edward IV popped his clogs prematurely, his two sons, Edward and Richard were sent to the Tower by Richard III for being bastards. However, whilst Edward was probably bumped off, Richard may have been spirited away to Europe somewhere.

At the Battle of Bosworth Field, Richard III was killed (and buried in a car park) and his army defeated by Henry VII. Chaos reigned and pretenders to the throne were two a penny with plenty of powerful individuals in both England and Europe willing to back a Yorkist claim to the throne.

Margaret of Burgundy was quite keen on reclaiming the throne (being the sister of Edward IV and Richard III and the aunt of the Princes in the Tower) and when this chap Warbeck turned up saying he was Richard she jumped at the chance of regaining power.

Richard/Perkin then went on a 'grand tour' attempting to garner support for his claim to be King and visited Ireland and then Scotland, both of which, having no love of the English, were keen to help. Unfortunately these alliances came to nought. However, the Cornish were cheesed off with the rest of the English, especially the tax regime at the time and when Richard pitched up there they welcomed him with open arms and even crowned him King Richard IV on Bodmin Moor.

Unfortunately, the Cornish attempt to take over the Country failed miserably. This didn't bode well for the then owner of Stowey Castle, Lord Audley, who backed the wrong side and had his head chopped off and his castle dismantled in retribution. Oh, and Perkin Warbeck, he confessed to being a Flemish apprentice who just happened to look like the dead prince.

Supposedly, in times gone by, the Mount was populated by giants who lived in underground caves and attempted to abduct passers-by. It was also the site of the original parish church, St Michaels, and villagers still erect a large wooden cross there every Easter. Other less salubrious uses include bear baiting, hen squalling (or cock fighting), bare knuckle fighting and shin kicking – well, they had to make their own entertainment in those days!

Before I left the Mount I activated my phone and saw that I was only 47 metres from the first instalment of Chris Jelley's fly catcher project and my phone soon buzzed with a poem to *Hartley Coleridge, Six Years Old'*. As I walked around the moat more of the poem appears. This is an interesting combination of modern technology and poetry from yesteryear.

Back en route Ozy and I headed downhill, and noticed the two gargoyle heads on Mount Cottage at the brow of the hill. These were probably taken from the original castle. I then passed by a pampered pet being groomed by Wendy and at the bottom of the hill is an honesty fruit and veg stall where in the summer you can pick up a piece of fruit for your journey. Some metropolitan visitors are astounded that people can still leave money by the roadside and no one steals it – ah! the joy of living in a really rural location.

Just around the corner, heading into Watery Lane, so called for reasons that soon become apparent, I stopped briefly to read another of Chris' poems before continuing along the track. This green lane gave me my first inkling of what to expect on this walk; quiet country lanes, gurgling streams and, as if on cue, a kingfisher flashed past, its iridescent blue catching my eye as it skimmed above the water.

Halfway along, the path became a stream but thoughtfully an alternative and higher path had been created so that I did not get wet. Ozy, however, preferred to paddle in the stream taking advantage of a free drink.

It's here that I encountered the next slate QR code attached to a fence post. The poems along the route were written by local schoolchildren and so I scanned this code and with a beep the poem appeared on my screen;

Barbed wire by the smelly old copper mine overgrown with wild garlic spreading its cloudy smell over the woods.
I see icicles dripping on the branch over the stream and buzzards gliding in the cold cloudy sky.

Halfway along this lane, just after the start of the elevated stretch, there are the remains of a building, down below on the left. No one knows what this was and the 1880 Ordnance Survey map doesn't show a building. Some say it was John Walford's house (more on this later).

During the spring this part of the track is covered in wild garlic or ramsons and the air is leaden with their pungent aroma. All parts of this plant are edible, although it is the leaves rather than the bulbs that are usually eaten, giving a much milder garlic flavour.

> Wild Garlic Pesto Recipe:
>
> 75g wild garlic leaves (chopped)
> 50g shelled walnuts
> 35g hard grated cheddar
> 125ml extra-virgin olive oil
> Fresh ground salt and pepper
>
> Put all the ingredients in a blender, adding the olive oil slowly until becoming a sloppy purée. Jar and refrigerate.

At the end of this lane is Broomsquires Cottage. Broomsquires were right at the bottom of society and made besom brooms from the beech twigs collected from Quantock Common, just a hundred yards or so further up the track. It is said that you could always tell a broomsquire by looking at their hands as they used blackberry twine to bind the twigs to the handle of the broom and stripped the thorns from the twine using their bare hands; therefore the palms of their hands were hard and leathery.

Villagers would have had commoners' rights to; keep pigs and take acorns and beech nuts (pannage), graze sheep (herbage or pasture), dig turf (turbary), dig for minerals (marl) and collect wood and gorse from the common (estover), which they could do by hook or by crook i.e. as long as they could pull down or break off branches rather than cut or chop them off.

Just behind the cottage, as I walked towards the ford, there is a small gravestone to 'Little Imp' who was killed by a motorcar in 1911.

Here Ozy and I turned right, steeply uphill, along Lucky Ike's Lane. No one is quite sure why Ike was lucky as I understand he had no legs. This was our first proper incline and it gave me some idea of what was to come over the next four days.

.

A GRUESOME MURDER AND A DRAGON

At the top of the lane I had arranged to meet local historian, David Worthy, who is 'Mr Quantock'. What David doesn't know about the Quantock Hills isn't worth knowing and he has written three learned tomes about the area together with a book on the Walford tragedy of 1789 and that's the reason that we are here today.

From the gate we looked into a large meadow towards the building straight ahead, the Counting House (occasionally hidden by trees). It was here that John Walford murdered his wife of three weeks. David takes over the story...

John Walford was a charcoal burner, not a particularly pleasant job as it involves spending a week at a time up in the Quantock Hills chopping down wood and then burning that wood under the cover of turf and in the absence of oxygen to create charcoal. The job was lonely, dirty and often bitterly cold with Walford complaining that his coat used to freeze on him in the long winter months.

Jane Shorney was "a poor stupid creature, almost an idiot; yet possessing a little kind of craftiness... an ordinary squat person, disgustingly dirty, and slovenly in her dress" (Tom Poole's words, not mine). A nice girl by all accounts! Whatever, Jane was in the habit of giving John 'comfort' on those long cold winter nights and as bitterly cold night followed not much warmer day, she became pregnant.

Now, being pregnant in eighteenth century England, and not being married, meant that the prospective mother was obliged to report her pregnancy to the local magistrate. The magistrate would then ask who the father was and in turn he would be called upon to support the child.

The father then had three rather stark choices; either he could marry the woman, put up a bastardy bond or go to jail – a case of hitched-up, pay-up or banged-up. In this case Walford's mother put up the money for a bastardy bond and this released him from his parental obligations.

Jane soon lost her interest in John and moved her attentions on to John's brother, William, who also managed to get her with child – definitely a case of keeping it in the family. However, it was not long before Jane was again visiting John to offer him comfort the following year. This time John was not in a position to put up the money for a bastardy bond and was therefore forced to marry Jane.

To complicate matters John had also managed to get pregnant his childhood sweetheart and only true love, Anne Rice. Therefore things weren't going too well for our John.

Fifteen days into the marriage in July 1789 Jane asked for a shilling to buy some cider from the Castle of Comfort, a cider house, a quarter of a mile from where David and I stood. We could see the route Jane would have taken with the remnants of the old copper mine in the distance. However, Jane never got her cider and was brutally murdered on her way to the inn.

The evidence against John was overwhelming and he was convicted of murder. The penalty for the offence was, of course, hanging and thereafter the judge directed that the body be used for medical science. However, the jury wanted to make an example of John and asked for him to be gibbeted - put in an iron cage to be a deterrent to other would-be wife killers. So John was hanged and then left in his iron cage 30 feet above the ground where the local wildlife could feed off his body – lovely!

David then told me an even more interesting and disturbing story about a walk he undertook with a chartered accountant friend of his some years ago.

David and his companion were walking from the main road up the coach road, that's the road circling round to our left. The friend, supposedly in tune with the spirit world, walked in the vicinity of the murder and, behind the Counting House, suddenly pulled out a small silver snuff box from his pocket and handed it to David. The box was hot, blisteringly hot, and there was no explanation for this.

A few weeks later when his companion opened the snuffbox he found that the paper inside had been burned to a cinder. David was convinced that this was where the murder was actually committed and his theory is that the ground, especially where there is a high iron content, remembers or records events. In this case the ground had replayed the events of that tragic day. I was not convinced, but it was a good story all the same.

It was time to move on as Ozy and I had another 13 miles to cover and we left David, walking steeply uphill over the body of Walford that still lay beneath our feet along the path. Some say that they have heard the chains of the gibbet rattling in the wind and can smell decaying flesh. Ozy and I didn't linger!

From the top of this field the remnants of Stowey's mining industry can be seen; the scar on the side of the hill is from open cast mining and looking across the A39 are the remnants of the Buckingham Copper Mine at Doddington. The Counting House, hidden amongst the trees at the north west corner of the field (just where Jane Shorney was murdered) was where the miners collected their wages.

Mining took place from the early eighteenth century with tin miners from Cornwall coming into the area. Copper ore was extracted as well as malachite, copper carbonate hydroxide, which was used as a green dye and paint up until about 1800 when synthetic greens were invented.

As a semi-precious gem stone, malachite is said to protect the wearer from accidents and safeguards travellers. Perhaps I should be wearing some on my walk? It also safeguards children and guards against undesirable business associations.

Due to the expense of operation and difficulties with ground water the mines closed in 1821.

At the top of the field, by the Walford's Gibbet signpost I reached the old coach road and headed up towards the Dukes Plantation named after the Duke of Buckingham who owned the land sometime in the fifteenth century.

The off-road track here is a little muddy but Ozy and I followed a beech hedge to the right with oaks on the left. These are Sessile oaks, originally managed for use in the tanning industry. These oaks differ from the classic English oak (Pedunculate) and can be told apart by the fact that these Quantock trees have acorns that are attached to the branch, rather than hanging down on stems.

Apart from the tannin used in the tannery, the bark was used as a dye, ink and had medicinal properties. The wood is strong and was used in ship-building, furniture and cabinet making. Food-wise, the acorns were loved by pigs, the sawdust was used for smoking and the wood for barrel and cask-making giving wine and spirits that oaky flavour.

Leaving the wood I was greeted by bright sunshine and gorse-lined open moorland with Dowsborough Hill on my left, climbing majestically and steeply to the Iron Age camp on the top. This is my adopted ancient monument here in the Quantocks.

A few years ago, English Heritage and the Quantocks AONB (Area of Outstanding Natural Beauty) asked for volunteers to record, monitor and generally look after the ancient monuments in the Quantocks, of which there are about 90.

I really wanted some tumuli or perhaps a knackered barrow which would be about the extent of my archaeological knowledge of the Iron Age period. When I went along to the 'adopt a monument at risk' day at the AONB offices in Fyne Court I held out for a couple of hummocks. But it was decreed that I would be allowed to look after Dowsborough. Now I climb the hill every couple of months to record its current state and pick up any litter dropped by uncaring visitors, and God help any mountain biker I find churning up the mud around the ramparts who is sent away with a park-keeper's authoritative flea in their ear.

The fort is Iron Age with ramparts and surrounding ditch. In the centre is a barrow, possibly older, dating back to the Bronze Age. Later it became connected to the Herepath and formed part of a series of forts used by King Alfred to warn of, and protect from, a Viking invasion. In fact the path from the fort is known as the Great Bear Path which is a corruption of Great Herepath.

Julius Caesar is said to have visited the fort and said "Quantum ad hoc" meaning "how much [I can see] from here." From this it was suggested we got the word 'Quantocks'. However, the far more likely explanation is that the name derives from the Saxon 'Cantuctun' meaning rim or circle.

The Domesday Book calls the area Cantoctona and Cantetone, again 'rim' or 'circle' with 'ton' or 'tun' meaning settlement.

Dowsborough is sometimes called Danesboro' by the locals although there is no historical evidence that the Danes had much of a hold in the area. However, some suggest that Wordsworth's 1799 poem, the *Danish Boy* took the idea and title from this location.

The Danish Boy walks here alone:

The lovely dell is all his own.

Luckily for us we are not required to traipse up to the fort and instead headed north up Woodlands Hill to the cairn at the top and its fantastic views of the north Somerset coast and south coast of Wales. Here I scanned the countryside for site of a copse of fir trees where a rather barbaric activity took place in years gone by.

It appears that on Good Friday each year boys from the local villages would meet at Fir Common to stone red squirrels to avenge the treachery of the red-headed Judas. The boys would try and knock the animals off the branches of the tall fir trees and the practice was known as 'hunting Judas'.

Whilst I was unable to locate the trees, probably having disappeared during the First World War, I couldn't miss the omnipresent Hinkley Point power station on the Bristol Channel.

Hinkley Point is in fact two power stations and soon to be three. The two squatter blue buildings are 'A' Station built in 1957 and no longer in use. Interestingly, the station was modified so that weapons-grade plutonium could be extracted for military purposes should the need arise.

Hinkley Point 'B' is the concrete coloured single building to the right and is an advanced gas-cooled reactor. It is still producing electricity and will continue to do so until the new 'C' Station is built. This will be a European pressurised reactor and is due to be completed in the early 2020s.

Swinging round from my vantage point there are two far more natural features, the islands of Steep Holm and Flat Holm in the middle of the Bristol Channel.

Steep Holm is the nearer and bigger of the two and lies about five miles offshore from Weston-super-Mare. The island is unpopulated and because of the tides, quite difficult to land on. It's a SSSI (Site of Special Scientific Interest) and a nature reserve covered in wild peony in the early summer. It's also home to the remains of a twelfth century Augustinian priory.

Whereas Steep Holm belongs to England the further and smaller of the two islands is Flat Holm and is part of Wales. This is the one with the lighthouse which was probably originally built by the Romans.

Again it is a SSSI but is habitable with its earliest visitor being St. Cadoc 'the Wise'. He was a frequent visitor to the island in the late sixth century where he went to meditate.

Legend has it that in the late twelfth century two of the murderers of Archbishop Thomas Becket were buried on the island. An archaeological dig a few years back supposedly found two graves that were aligned north to south rather than the normal east-west and carbon dating suggests these were from the twelfth century, so there may be some truth in the legend.

Being situated in the middle of the Bristol Channel, the island made a perfect base for smuggling with plenty of old mineshafts and tunnels for a quick escape should the customs' men come a-calling. The most famous of these smugglers was Pasco Robinson who, in the early eighteenth century, sailed his ship with red mermaid figurehead, seemingly untouchable by the authorities.

It was also here that in 1897 Marconi, and his Welsh assistant, George Kemp, transmitted the first wireless signals over open sea from Flat Holm to Lavernock Point near Penarth. It always astounds me that words spoken at times of momentous historical significance are often poorly planned. For instance, Neil Armstrong supposedly ad-libbed his "one giant step" speech. In this case Marconi's first words were "Are you ready"!

For those of you who are fans of Doctor Who or Torchwood, episodes where deserted military establishments are required have been filmed there, being just a stone's throw from Cardiff. The island also has its own pub, 'The Gull and Leek', the most southerly pub in Wales, and you can even stay overnight.

Back to the walk... around the cairn is evidence of the bracken having been burnt. This is the result of 'swaling' and encourages the regeneration of vegetation. I always get the impression that the AONB rangers really enjoy this part of their job - as have pyromaniacs for thousands of years!

And now downhill again. At a meeting of paths there is Shervage Wood to my right. This is the home of the infamous 'Gurt Vurm' (Great Worm). There be dragons in this neck of the woods you see!

The story goes that at the Triscombe Revel, an annual Quantocks fair, an old lady sold whortleberry tarts (see later for details on these – whortleberries, not the tarts!). These were said to be bewitched as it was impossible to just eat one and you had to have another and another…

This old lady used to collect her whortleberries from Shervage Wood, however, the Gurt Vurm had taken up residence and was making a nuisance of itself by eating sheep, cattle and horses. Anyone who went up into the woods suffered a similar fate and the charred clothes of the odd squire had been found on the hillside.

One September day, the old woman was distraught. She could smell the whorts, but couldn't collect them for fear of being eaten by the dragon, when by chance a young woodcutter from Stogursey arrived. Stogursey is a village about three miles away and therefore blissfully unaware of the rampaging dragon (people don't travel too much hereabouts).

The old woman spun some yarn about being too old to collect the whortleberries and the young man volunteered to do so for her. Using his woodcutters' chopper he cleared the banks of the hill to collect the berries and on coming across a particularly robust tree trunk went at it with enthusiasm. However, it was not a log he was chopping but the Gurt Vurm itself. So vigorous was the man with his chopper that he chopped the dragon in half, with both halves slithering away in opposite directions, forming the Quantock Hills. And that's why you should always close gates when walking on the Quantocks to stop the two halves of the dragon being able to join up again.

Of course the story has a factual basis in that the beach at Kilve and the surrounding inland area contained the remains of fossilised creatures, many of which could be mistaken for a dragon.

The wood also has its own ghost and at midnight on Christmas Eve a coach pulled by four black horses takes the road between Holford and Nether Stowey. Luckily it was not Christmas!

DIRECTIONS

NETHER STOWEY TO HOLFORD

From Coleridge Cottage head into the centre of the village and turn right into Castle Street at the Cross. Continue up Castle Hill and at the top detour right to the Castle Mount. Return to Castle Hill and walk down to a T junction, turn left here and after 100 yards turn right into Watery Lane. At Broomsquires Cottage, turn right up Lucky Ikes Lane. At the top of the lane, go through the gate and head uphill to follow the left-hand field boundary aiming for the left of an old mining scar on the hillside. At the top of the field exit through a gate and continue straight ahead, up the road.

After 600 yards turn right along a sunken green track, taking the slightly higher ground to the left if too muddy. Enter into open moorland and after 400 yards, at a T junction, turn right up Woodlands Hill, then down the other side into woodland. At the road turn left uphill along the road. At the Triangle, turn right signposted 'Car Park 250 yards'. At the Silk Mills signpost turn sharp left towards the car park to the Bowling Green.

HOLFORD AND ROBIN HOOD

As I reached the road and turned right uphill, I took the old road which originally crossed the river where the thatched cottages now are. This was the original 'Holeford'.

There has been a settlement here since the Romans and coinage has been found bearing the head of Constantine. Probably the Romans used Dowsborough as a summer camp, a bit like Butlins today!

The village was originally a centre for tanning, like Nether Stowey. There were nine tanyards in the area, including the building where the Combe House Hotel now stands, a few hundred yards to the west of 'The Triangle' signpost - worth a look for the huge water wheel that powered the tannery machinery and also generated electricity in 1900 for the building and surrounding cottages.

The woods surrounding the combes (Holford and Hodders) were managed and coppiced and cut in rotation every 40 years with the bark, again being used in the tanning process. The wood itself was often used for charcoal and this was made into gunpowder for the Royal Navy.

The church, which can be seen from the top of the old road, is St Marys, either the Blessed Virgin or Magdalene, there is some debate. However, the original church was Saxon. The present building was reconstructed in the 1840s.

This was to be my next stop, not for any religious reason but the fact that I am meeting a local cider producer there.

Ian Cunneen is the proprietor of Mad Apple Cider, based in Holford. He also looks as if he has just stepped out of the set for a new Lord of the Rings film with his wayward pointed beard and whiskers, bleached blonde no doubt by the hot Somerset sun or acidic cider fumes, his hobbit hat, braces and pot belly. However, what Ian doesn't know about cider isn't worth knowing.

I'm not quite sure of the etiquette of drinking on hallowed ground but as the weather is beautiful, I thought it would be safe to sit outside without offending too many people.

Ian had brought with him three mini-pins of cider, a dry, medium and sweet and we started with the dry. This is pure fermented apple juice with nothing added or taken away just apple juice and yeast. Now, I am not an expert in these things, but the cider tasted perfect... sitting in a graveyard... in the sun.

Ian told me that he has perfected the sophisticated art of apple collection by shaking trees and banging them with a long stick. This is a proper artisan product, made and sold locally with passion and enthusiasm.

Having knocked back the dry I next tried the medium. This has had a natural sweetener added to it, a herb called 'stevia', which has the advantage of not being fermentable. The problem with adding normal sugar to sweeten a natural cider, is the yeast just eats up the sugar and converts it into additional alcohol. Ian said that he tried growing stevia, but with limited success – it died, so he now uses a prepared product, gauging how much to add to each batch.

The cider is now having a very relaxing effect and I am slumped slightly on the churchyard bench. Time for the sweet I thought.

The sweet cider contains more stevia and is as palatable as the others and as alcoholic. Ian is obviously used to drinking his cider as he seems to be fine. He told me that half a pint of cider provides a similar amount of antioxidants as drinking a glass of red wine, protecting you from all manner of nasty diseases. Captain Cook even took it aboard his ships as an effective treatment for scurvy.

In the past cider was considered part of a labourer's wage, continuing well into the twentieth century even though the Truck Act of 1887 made it illegal to pay wages in beer or cider. Having now consumed three tankards of the local ambrosia, I find it difficult to imagine how anyone could do any work after drinking this stuff, but work, or walk in my case, is what I must do and I say goodbye to Ian and head off to the pub.

Just down the road from the church is the Plough Inn. This former coaching inn is a lovely spot for a refreshing pint and on a fine day the garden is beautiful.

Virginia Woolf and her husband, Leonard, spent their honeymoon in the pub in 1912 and revisited a year later for Virginia to recover from some psychological problems. Leonard later wrote; 'The people who kept it were pure Holford folk. The food was delicious. Nothing could be better than the bread, butter, cream and eggs and bacon of the Somersetshire breakfast with which you begin your morning'.

I'm not sure what 'Holford folk' are like but Chris at the Plough does a very nice all day breakfast sandwich!

The Plough is rumoured to be haunted by the ghost of a Spanish merchant who stayed there in November 1555 on his way back to Bristol after trading in the South West. This was a time of great mistrust of Spaniards with the Tudors thinking they were all spies. This particular individual may well have boasted about all the gold he had acquired from his successful trading and was consequently robbed and stabbed to death. His ghost can be seen in a dark cape walking the stairs.

Roger Evans, the author of *Somerset Stories of the Supernatural*, tells a somewhat more tongue in cheek ghost story about the pub (albeit that the location of the pub differs depending on where Roger gives his talks).

Supposedly, the pub had a very friendly cat that was loved by all the regulars. However, one dark and stormy night the cat went out and was unfortunately run over by a passing Land Rover on the A39. The regulars were distraught and wanted the poor animal to be stuffed by a local taxidermist.

However, the wheels of the Land Rover being big and the cat being small, there was little left to be stuffed and only the tail was suitable for mounting and duly hung behind the bar.

A few weeks later whilst the landlord was clearing up at closing time he spotted a movement out of the corner of his eye and there was the cat, sans tail. The cat explained (yes it talked) that it was unable to pass over to the other side without its tail and asked if it could have it back. The landlord replied that since it was after eleven o'clock he was unable to 'retail spirits'.

Groan.

Full of tales of ghostly happenings as well as beer and cider, I headed off with Ozy to re-join the path.

At Silk Mills I peered over the wall opposite into Holford Glen. Here there are the ruins of an old late sixteenth century building. This was originally a fulling mill (the process of taking out the oils, dirt, and other impurities and making the woollen cloth thicker) built by Calvinist Huguenots fleeing religious persecution in Europe. It later became a silk mill, although there is some debate as to when this occurred as mechanised silk mills were a relatively modern, eighteenth century, invention. The silk worms were hatched in Over Stowey, no doubt on mulberry bushes.

The eighteenth century remains are surrounded by beech, oak, ash, sycamore, elm, scots pine and larch trees and a beautiful woodland glen. This is probably the site of Dorothy Wordsworth's 'low damp dell' appearing in her 8th February 1798 diary entry as follows;

Walked to Woodlands, and to the waterfall. The adder's-tongue and the ferns green in the low damp dell. These plants now in perpetual motion from the current of the air; in summer only moved by the drippings of the rocks. A cloudy day.

However, of even greater artistic importance is the fact that the site was the backdrop for the Canadian singer, Bryan Adams' music video *(Everything I do) I do it for you*, the soundtrack to the film *Robin Hood Prince of Thieves*. I have brought my multi-media tablet with me just to relive the experience – oh and there's the mill and the lovely Bryan… and people are staring at me,… and I'm now feeling nauseous.

I wonder if it's still number one?

Kevin Costner even came here for the filming, but a search of the trees has not yet revealed a Bryan♥Kevin carving.

However, we needed to get on along the path and soon reach an expanse of grass known as the Bowling Green, or more probably the *boules* green as the area was used by the Huguenots to play their home game.

Just past the green, on the corner is a dog pound and I could just make out the crest of the St Albyn's family in the top circle, the owners of Alfoxton in the fifteenth century. It's a wolf – not a dog. The track to the left of the dog pound is the original old road which headed up over Longstone Hill.

Legend has it that the hunting hounds for the estate were housed nearby and their meat was hung on trees, known as 'pantry trees'. Not surprisingly, the smell of food attracted the local stray dogs and on one particular night these strays were unsettling the hunt dogs. The huntsman went out to calm his dogs down, but rather than wearing his normal hunting gear he was dressed in his civvies. Unfortunately, the hounds did not recognise him and tore him to bits! This is the sort of disaster that spurs people into action, albeit rather late in the day, and the village then built the dog pound I saw today.

It is this huntsman who is said to have inspired Wordsworth's poem, *Simon Lee: The Old Huntsman* which begins

In the sweet shire of Cardigan,
Not far from pleasant Ivor-hall,
An old Man dwells...

Whilst this poem mentions 'Cardigan' it is based on Christopher Tricky a contemporary of Wordsworth who lived in a small cottage opposite the gates of Alfoxton Park.

The road now took us towards Alfoxton Park, once the home of William and Dorothy Wordsworth and, just before entering the estate, I saw movement out of the corner of my eye and noticed that the field to the right is full of red deer going about their business.

Alfoxton House, also known as Alfoxton Park, was built as an 18th-century country house and it was here that William Wordsworth and his sister Dorothy lived from July 1797 to June 1798 at the behest of Coleridge and with the help of Tom Poole who persuaded the St. Albyn Family to let them rent the house for the princely sum of £23 a year.

Here Dorothy wrote a journal for a couple of months and said in this;

Here we are in a large mansion, in a large park with seventy head of deer around us. There is furniture enough for a dozen families like ours. There is an excellent garden, well stocked with vegetables and fruit. The front of the house is to the south, but it is screened from the sun by a high hill. From the end of the house we have a view of the sea.

Coleridge spent a great deal of time here at Alfoxton both conversing and walking with William and Dorothy. This must have caused Sara added anxiety, especially given the fact that Coleridge thought Dorothy to have a superior intellect, "She is a woman indeed" said STC, qualifying the comment by adding, "…in mind I mean."

There has been much speculation about whether Coleridge did, in fact, have a sexual relationship with Dorothy. However, if they did they kept it very quiet.

However, the Wordsworths' time there, even surrounded by good friends, was not particularly contented due to the somewhat hostile reception given to them by the locals and it was here that their houseman reported them to the authorities as potential French spies; going out along the Bristol Channel, to untrodden places, late at night, no doubt signalling to fleets of enemy ships waiting to invade.

Whilst the Wordsworths may not have been welcomed with open arms they loved the Quantocks all the same and William discovered his 'new creative drive' enabling him to describe the nature around him, penning;

of olive green and scarlet bright
in spikes, in branches and in stars,
green red and pearly white

about a thorn.

Perhaps somewhat less charitable was his poem, *The Idiot Boy* about a lad called Simon Lee who lived in Nether Stowey. The poor chap is a bit of a simpleton going around saying: "The cocks did crow, and the moon did shine so cold."

And Johnny burrs, and laughs aloud;

47

Whether in cunning or in joy
I cannot tell; but while he laughs,
Betty a drunken pleasure quaffs
To hear again her Idiot Boy.

Since the Wordsworths left, the house has had many uses and in 1943 became a field hospital as part of the preparations and build up to D-Day.

Today the house is a shadow of its former self and in a state of some disrepair. Such a shame.

The path now took Ozy and I along the north side of the Quantocks to skirt round the many combes that run south/north off the hills, many of which are loved by mountain bikers who career downhill; some of whom are miraculously still attached to their bikes at the bottom.

The Quantocks form part of Mountain Bike Rider Magazine's 'Killer Loops' and from my understanding of the routes, are not for the faint-hearted or skinny tyres. Riders describe the downhill treks as 'mini canyons of rock' and a 'final hurtle' and the uphill bits as 'evil'. Whatever, it pays to keep an eye open for these hare-brained men and women and to give them a wide berth as stopping might be difficult.

We were also back in open moorland again surrounded by gorse, heather and bracken reminding me of why I am wearing long trousers for this trip. Whilst I don't want to worry anyone, there are ticks in these here hills. These are little spider-like parasites that can burrow into exposed skin. They carry a bacterium that can lead to Lyme Disease, which can be a bit nasty if left untreated. However, the symptoms are easyish to spot; a rash with a centre spot and an outer red ring, looking a bit like a bull's eye, about five centimetres in diameter. This may be accompanied by flu-like symptoms and these are only likely to be experienced after the walk, so don't worry too much about anything until you get home, but don't forget that you were bitten if you feel unwell a few weeks later!

My tip for avoiding these nasty little bugs; wear long trousers and tuck them into socks if walking through bracken and gorse, avoid walking through the undergrowth to start with and check to make sure one hasn't attached itself to you at the end of the day.

Ozy, however, is another matter and after a day's walk it is not unusual to find a tick or two on him and his 'tick tweezers' are in my rucksack just in case.

Lucky dog!

DIRECTIONS

HOLFORD TO WEST QUANTOXHEAD

From the car park, pass the bowling green on your left heading along the road straight ahead and at the dog pound swing round to the right. Follow the estate drive past Alfoxton House on your left and head uphill on the tarmac road zig-zagging uphill. Pass through the hamlet with the road becoming a wide track heading downhill. At the T junction, turn left, signposted to Perry. Continue in this direction for a couple of miles, climbing and descending into combes and crossing streams. Keep following signs to Perry and ignore those to the A39.

At a Quantock Greenway post with a number of signs, including a West Somerset Coast Path 'ammonite' sign, take either the left bridleway or right permissive path, the latter being less steep. Enter into the woods by way of a kissing gate. On meeting a forestry track, turn right, initially downhill.

Now follow signs to West Quantoxhead. The track travels up and then snakes down gently after the bench at the top. After the short wooded area, turn right towards the road. At the A39 take the footpath parallel to the main road and use the drive of the Windmill pub.

ST AUDREY AND A MERMAID

My next stop was West Quantoxhead and I saw the St Audries estate initially from above. In the distance I saw Exmoor and Dunkery Hill where Ozy and I would be in a couple of days' time.

A buzzard circled overhead, keening, using the thermal currents to lazily hunt for prey. The buzzard is the emblem of the Quantock Hills and Britain's commonest bird of prey.

The St Audries estate was originally the village itself, situated along the drive to the church and manor. Today the village of West Quantoxhead is further along the main road and was formed by Act of Parliament in 1828 for the Minehead Turnpike Trust. The Coleridge Way does not pass through the current village, although there is a shop for basic provisions at the petrol station just past the turning for Bicknoller.

St Audries manor has had a number of uses since being built as the Acland family home. It has been a private girls school, a Buddhist retreat and is now a wedding venue.

The name, West Quantoxhead comes from a mixture of old English and celtic and was originally Cantocheve Minor or 'hill country head'. The 'Major' parish is East Quantoxhead a few miles down the road. Both are recorded in the Domesday Book of 1085.

The present church was built in 1854, replacing a dilapidated medieval building. In fact, the original church may not have had to be demolished if it was not for the fact that in 1800 the church wardens bought 10,500 roof tiles at the exorbitant cost of four guineas. Unfortunately, these tiles were too heavy for the building causing it to collapse.

St Audrey (or Etheldreda) was Queen of Northumbria who became the first abbess of Ely. Audrey died in 679AD from a tumour of the throat. She put this down to a fondness for necklaces as a younger woman and this was her punishment from God. Interestingly we get the word 'tawdry', from her name coming from the fact that followers of the saint bought pieces of lace at Ely market to cover up their décolletage (neck, shoulders and chest to you and me). However, by the seventeenth century such lacework was deemed to be old fashioned and the Puritans decried any form of unnecessary decoration as ungodly, hence such adornments being 'tawdry'.

Ozy could see the Bristol Channel from our vantage point and looked longingly at it. However, I warned him sternly of the dangers of this particular coastline and, in particular, the story of the Sea Morgan's Child.

Legend has it that a fisherman went down to the beach at St Audries in the owl light (twilight) to fish but the tide was out. He was just about to go home when he heard the sound of singing above the noise of the waves. Silently, he crept towards the haunting music and saw a group of sea morgans (mermaids or sirens) combing their hair with razor shells.

Even though the fisherman was tiptoeing silently he stumbled and frightened the sea maidens who slipped back into the sea. However, in their hurry to get away from the fisherman they inadvertently left one of their young behind, a beautiful girl child.

The fisherman picked up the child and took her home to his wife. The couple decided to bring up the child as their own and named her Morgan.

The girl, now being a creature of the land, failed to grow a fish tail and in every way looked like a human apart from the fact that her hair never dried, smelled of the sea and she was obsessed by all water; the child could never pass a pond or stream or even a bird bath without trailing her hand though the liquid.

The girl grew up, as they tend to do, and her strange antics caught the attention of the local busybodies who noticed that Morgan would never attend church and preferred splashing about in the millpond. This together with her constantly wet hair, beautiful singing voice and un-Christian name started to cause concern.

Then one day, music and singing was heard from the bay. Both the fisherman and Morgan heard this and Morgan said. "They are calling me now – there'll be a storm tonight", and with that she was gone – back with her own kind, never to be seen again.

And there was a storm, one of the worst in living memory.

After hearing the story, Ozy decided that it may not be a good idea to go swimming and we passed The Windmill pub (Ozy wasn't allowed in; the only pub along the whole 51 mile route) and turned off the A39.

After a bit more road work we skirted round the western side of the hills and into woodland with views of the Brendons to our right. We travelled up and down combes, some quite steep and passed by

Weacombe before reaching the pretty village of Bicknoller and its community shop. Handy if you need more poo bags for Ozy – good planning, bad packing!

Bicknoller may be named after '*the alder trees of a man called Bica*' or '*little Treasure*', but no one is quite sure.

As it was lunchtime I decided to stop off at the Bicknoller Inn, affectionately known as *The Bick*. This is not actually on the route and I wasn't quite sure why this was. However, it was a lovely day and Ozy and I sat in the secluded cobbled courtyard surrounded by fragrant hanging baskets, sharing a sandwich with Ozy which I washed down with a pint of Palmers IPA.

Whilst I could have sat there all afternoon, we had a good few miles to cover and we headed off, crossing the A358 Taunton to Williton road, almost immediately meeting the tracks of the West Somerset Railway.

DIRECTIONS

WEST QUANTOXHEAD TO SAMPFORD BRETT

From The Windmill pub turn immediately left along The Avenue signposted Bicknoller and Taunton. At Staple Cross continue straight ahead along Weacombe Road. After 400 yards, opposite Leighway, turn left to double back on yourself along a metalled path and head up right into the woods.

After ¼ mile, exit through the gate and turn right, immediately through a second gate. Just after the first house on the right turn left to cross a stream over a couple of railway sleepers. Go through the gate and into woods again. After a steep descent cross a stream and turn right down a forest track. At a five bar wooden gate continue straight ahead along a narrow tarmac road and after 400 yards enter Bicknoller.

Head down Dashwoods Lane [The Bicknoller Inn lies down Gatchells Lane and to the right]. On reaching the A358 cross over and continue straight ahead along a gated green lane, joining the McMillan Way.

Ignore the stile at the farm buildings and turn right along the green lane. Cross the railway line and head along the woodland path straight ahead. Then over a stile, into a field, keeping a field boundary to your left. Continue into the next field and then turn left to join a farm track. Turn right here.

Continue to the road and turn left, over a bridge. On meeting a Somerset County Council (SCC) signpost where the road bends round to the left, turn right here NOTE; there is no CW signage here. This is signposted Capton and Sampford Brett. After 50 yards keep straight ahead, enter a farmyard and a track between two farm buildings. After 400 yards, take a footpath by a kissing gate on the right and take the path straight ahead through the field. Exit the field through a further kissing gate and follow a woodland path, then follow the stream and lane into Sampford Brett. Continue straight ahead towards the church.

WOODLAND SPIRITS

Sampford Brett is a quiet and pleasant village (their words not mine) with pretty little bridges over the brook but there was little to keep us there and with a bit of time to spare I decided to take a detour to have a look at Williton, just fifteen minutes up the road.

This is a small town with all major amenities; bank, supermarket, petrol station and is also the administrative centre of West Somerset Council. It has a number of B&Bs and pubs and would be an ideal overnight stop for those wanting a shorter first day's walking.

As we passed the Wyndam Arms I noticed it was open and deciding that it would be churlish to ignore this obvious invitation, and because it is dog friendly, Ozy and I popped in for a beer (and bowl of water) and joined the solitary regulars nursing their pints. This is a pub that had resisted any attempts at modernisation and was a town 'boozer' serving good beer and basic pub grub.

Back on the trail, our night's destination was not too far off and we headed towards Aller reaching a little wooden bridge with a curious sign reading;

In ancient times it was considered prudent for travellers about to cross a wooden bridge to make an offering to the spirits of the trees which were cut to provide the timber. Unless a thief or destitute person has taken it, you will find a small coin on one of the pillars, please carry it across and place it on the pillar on the opposite side so that the next traveller may use it to cross safely. If all the coins have been taken you may wish to leave a small token to aid those who come after you.

Aller Farm itself is pretty with its cliff garden created from a three-sided quarry containing old magnolia, fig and Judas trees.

Looking due north I could see into south Wales and the Vale of Glamorgan with Aberthaw Power Station at Barry stark against the coast – a blot on the landscape, which is probably what the Welsh say when they look over and see Hinkley Point on our side.

As we neared Monksilver we travelled along a sunken path with ancient hedges either side and badger sets very much in evidence. Counting the number of tree species in a hedgerow, known as the *ancient woodland indicator,* can give some idea of how old the hedge is with many trees taking a century to be established. So count the number of dominant species and multiply by a hundred to get an age. I counted four.

West Somerset is also one of the areas trialling a controversial badger cull to halt the spread of bovine tuberculosis which is having a devastating effect on cattle in the area that graze on open ground. This topic can cause many a heated argument and I shall, wisely, keep out of it.

DIRECTIONS

SAMPFORD BRETT TO MONKSILVER

At the church turn left through the village past the red telephone box. At a junction, take the road on the right, but immediately head straight on, past a no entry sign at Clowder Cottage (number 7). After 100 yards turn right at Manor Farm, through the farmyard and exit along a green lane. Follow the right hand field boundary between the fence and the hedge, following a stream. Cross the stream and briefly head uphill, then at a T junction, turn left. Cross the bridge (remembering to pay your penny to do so). Turn right at farm buildings, passing between them. At the track junction, turn left, passing a number of barns.

Skirt around four large fields and in the corner of the last field exit the field on to a woodland path, turning left along a sunken woodland track. After about a mile and on meeting a road continue straight ahead along the road, ignoring the signpost to Monksilver ¼ mile.

After 400 yards and as the road bends round to the left. Continue straight ahead along a green track. After just under ½ mile and on reaching wooden steps on the left, turn right and go through a metal gate. Keep to the left hand field boundary through three fields. On meeting the road, turn right signposted to Williton, Watchet and Minehead (B3188). Head into the village and towards the Notley Arms.

MONKSILVER AND THE DENTIST GARGOYLE

And so we reached our destination for our first day, Monksilver and the Notley Arms.

The pub has had a bit of a chequered history recently resulting in it becoming the UK's first listed 'community asset' by West Somerset Council after threats to turn it into a private dwelling. However, it now appears to be in safe hands with Simon and Caroline Murphy owning it and it was Simon who greeted me on arrival.

After a wash and brush-up I sat at the bar looking forward to a quiet pint and a relaxing evening. However, this was not to be as tonight was the annual get-together of the Stogumber Church Choir with their vicar, Val.

Val, and I'm sure that she has heard this a thousand times, looks just like Geraldine Granger/Kennedy from the BBC sitcom, The Vicar of Dibley. Not only that, she acts a bit like Geraldine with her mobile phone ringtone calling out "This is a message from God" whenever she receives a text!

The choir were in fine voice and I was treated to a specially adapted rendition of *All Things Bright and Beautiful* going something like this;

> *We are in Stogumber Choir*
> *All singers of renown*
> *The sops and tenors sing right up*
> *The others sing right down.*

The hymn, in its original form, has an association with the area. Throughout this stretch of the walk I have had views of Minehead and just to the south east, Dunster. It was in Minehead that Cecil F Alexander wrote *All Things Bright and Beautiful* and 'the purple headed mountain and river running by' is likely to be about Grabbist Hill and the River Avill to the west of Dunster.

However, and perhaps more controversially, is the fact that Mrs Alexander (yes, she's a she) may have plagiarised the wording for the hymn from none other than Samuel Taylor Coleridge himself. Consider this stanza from the *Ancient Mariner...*

> *He prayeth best, who loveth best*
> *All things both great and small;*
> *For the dear God who loveth us*
> *He made and loveth all.*

...and tell me that these are not the same!

And so to bed, tired and replete, looking forward to the next stretch of the Coleridge Way. Oh, and now I can't get that confounded hymn out of my head!

*****

I woke up to a beautiful day and felt fully refreshed – ish. It can't have been the beer; it must have been all that singing!

Whilst I was now technically out of the Quantocks and now on Exmoor I met Chris Edwards the manager of the Quantocks AONB for a chat about the area and his work. Chris has been working at the AONB for eleven years and knows the hills like the back of his hand.

Areas of Outstanding Natural Beauty are English, Northern Irish and Welsh regions designated for conservation due to their significant landscape value. They are similar to National Parks but do not have their own governing bodies. Their purpose is to conserve and enhance the landscape, allowing quiet enjoyment for visitors whilst respecting those who live and work within the defined boundaries.

The idea for AONBs was formed in 1945 when it was suggested that there was a need to protect certain naturally beautiful landscapes but due to size or lack of 'wilderness' they were not suitable to be National Parks. The Quantock Hills were England's first AONB, being designated in 1956, and Chris is very proud of this fact.

The Quantocks AONB has its headquarters at Fyne Court in the heart of the Quantock Hills and shares its home with the National Trust. The house was originally built in 1629, surrounded by plantations but burnt down in 1894. Whilst little of the building remains, the stories that the old house could tell are extraordinary.

The house was originally owned by the Crosse family and the most famous member was Andrew Crosse, known as the 'Thunder and Lightning Man' after conducting a series of experiments with electricity in the early nineteenth century. Crosse erected 'an extensive apparatus for examining the electricity of the atmosphere' where he 'collected' lightning by stringing wires from the house and around the nearby trees. Sir Humphry Davy visited Crosse in 1827 and the two of them were at the forefront of the development of large voltaic piles or basic batteries.

However, his life was to take an unexpected turn when in 1836 he was experimenting in electrocrystallization, passing a current through volcanic rocks, when he observed the 'creation' of tiny mites. The effect of his experiments should have been to destroy any living matter, but mites there were.

Crosse was very fastidious when recording data and passed no judgment on the event merely identifying it as a scientific anomaly. However, others were more than happy to comment and the 'extraordinary experiment' appeared in the Somerset County Gazette and, reprinted by newspapers across Europe, made Crosse's discovery famous.

Unfortunately, given that this was a period when religion was an important part of most people's lives, and the fact that the press had suggested that the scientist had 'created life' and was 'playing at God', the incident did not go down well.

There is one lasting outcome of this event. Crosse gave a lecture in London on his findings and in the audience were (or so it is claimed) Mary and Percy Bysshe Shelley. It is this lecture that supposedly inspired Mary Shelley to write Frankenstein.

So with gothic novels on our mind and after a full-on breakfast Ozy and I set off on Day Two of our walk.

Monksilver means the monk's wood from the latin *silva* meaning 'an area of woodland'. It is mentioned in the Domesday Book in 1086 and is called *Selvre* and *Selui* there, just meaning 'wood'. At the time the manor was held by Alured d'Epaignes and the church guide translates this as 'the Spaniard' although this has to be the same Alfred d'Epaignes who owned Nether Stowey Castle and who came from Normandy.

Alured or Alfred's daughter Isabel married Robert de Chandos and it was Robert who annexed part of Monmouthshire (in Wales) to Norman England and then founded Goldcliff Priory in Newport, endowing it with the proceeds from the area surrounding Monksilver.

It initially seemed strange to me that a priory in Monmouthshire should be attached to property in west Somerset, but then it's not that far by sea and with Watchet just up the road, the journey would have been relatively short.

Robert was then persuaded by Henry I to give his priory to the Benedictine Abbaye du Bec-Hellouin in Normandy which was the most influential abbey in the Anglo-Norman kingdom in the twelfth century. Again this seems odd until you realise that Henry I was William the Conqueror's son and that the Archbishop of Canterbury was Theobald of Bec.

Once under the control of the Abbaye du Bec twelve monks were sent from France to run Monksilver Abbey and the church guide speculates that perhaps stonemasons were also sent from Normandy to build the church.

Jump forward to the 1440s and Tewskesbury Abbey benefited from the wealth of the village followed by Eton College in 1475. In modern times the whole village was bought by the Reverend George Notley who became lord of the manor, hence the name of the pub.

As I strode out on our second day I immediately got lost. The directions here seemed to be wrong as the path taken by the guide seems to be the bridle path rather than the walkers' path, the latter taking us past the church.

So I headed up from the pub car park into the church of All Saints. I love looking in country churches, although Ozy's not so keen, getting bored easily. However, it's the outside of this church which interested me. As I looked up, just above the flat-topped window, there was a gargoyle - supposedly being the first representation of a dentist. Technically it's not a gargoyle as gargoyles are carvings used to disguise water spouts, guttering or drains (and this was not), but it looked like a gargoyle to me.

Supposedly, it's a representation of Bishop Button of Bath and Wells who is the patron saint of toothache sufferers. And here's a free fact for any pub quiz compilers; "when is National Toothache Day?" Answer, 9th February! The 10th is National Umbrella Day and the 11th ...Don't Cry Over Spilled Milk Day. Honestly, look it up!

THE BRENDONS AND A LOT OF UP

So I left Monksilver and according to the map the next section had a great many contours and they are close together meaning a steep section.

Bird's Hill is a mile and a half long and is a very slow climb out of the village. This is a challenge, especially after a very large full English breakfast.

Normally hikers walk at about three miles (or five kilometres) an hour. However, this will change depending on the degree of climb or descent. This is known as Naismith's rule, a Scottish mountaineer who devised it in 1892.

The rule is based on walkers of reasonable fitness, on typical terrain, under normal conditions. Not Scotland then!

In addition, so says Naismith, the dynamics of any party must be taken into consideration including walking at the speed of the slowest person (which is the opposite of drinking rounds in pubs which are governed by the fastest drinker). Ozy is the fastest walker having four legs and a stomach which is not full of sausage and bacon. I am the slowest having only two legs, a stomach full of sausage and bacon, loads of toast and a slight hangover.

Bird's Hill is up with uneven terrain. For the uneven bit the amount of ground covered is reduced by 20%. For the up bit (over 12% incline) I need to add ten minutes per 1,000 feet of up... Then there's Tranter's fatigue factor...

The best bit is that the calculations are both in metric and imperial making any calculation impossible. All I can say is that it's a tiresome and long climb and I was very pleased to get to the top. Having said that the flora during our climb took my mind off the trudge with bluebells, pink campion, wood anemones and foxgloves in amongst the beech and oak woodland.

According to the Ordnance Survey map we were now in the centre of the Brendon Hills. These tend to get neglected, being sandwiched between the Quantocks AONB and Exmoor National Park, although they form part of the Park for administration purposes. It is perhaps because the Brendons are more cultivated and have seen more agricultural activity over the last century than their next door neighbours that they tend to get second billing and have fewer leisure visitors.

The name 'Brendon' is a combination of Bruna or Brune, meaning 'brown' and 'dun' is old English for a fairly flat and extensive hill. Not a very inspiring combination, but lovely for all that.

At the top of Bird's Hill I reached Colton Cross with tantalising glimpses of the coast through the trees as I walked along the road. At a permissive path sign I took a detour to a view-point and on top of a small mound had a magnificent 180 degree panorama to the north, only spoiled by the twin radio and television aerials at Tropiquaria at Washford Cross.

However, far more interesting is Nettlecombe Court in its own secluded valley down below me. The present house was originally a Tudor mansion with Georgian additions in 150 acres of grounds.

Nettlecombe has never been bought or sold. It was held by Prince Godwine, son of King Harold before 1066 and then came into the ownership of William the Conqueror after the battle. In 1160, Henry II granted it to Hugh de Raleigh, and it stayed in the same family, through marriage, until the nineteenth century.

The house has seen many alterations and enlargements over the centuries, some caused by fire including the burning down of part of the property by Roundheads opposed to George Trevelyan's support of the monarchy during the English Civil War.

In the nineteenth century, Lady Trevelyan invited members of the Pre-Raphaelite Brotherhood to use the property. These were a group of English artists and poets most famous for paintings of nature, romance and medieval revivalism – you know the stuff; half naked, wan and dreamy women floating in ponds and the like.

Most recently, it has been a field study centre for those wanting to study the local natural environment, including; marine, freshwater and heather moorland areas and also archaeological excavations nearby.

Of course, fiction trumps fact for the most interesting stories and the Trevelyan coat of arms depicts a horse rising out from the sea and this is part of the Lyonesse legend.

The Lyonesse were lands belonging to King Arthur and the Castle of Camelot and the site of the final mortal battle between Arthur and Mordred. These lands were submerged beneath the sea hence why King Arthur's body has never been discovered. Only one knight from the Round Table survived the inundation of the sea and this was Trevelyan, who escaped by riding his white horse through the rising waters – hence the horse on the coat of arms.

The Lyonesse was also the home of Tristan and Isolde, the main characters in the medieval love triangle story. Even the Romans got in on the act with a sunken kingdom by the name of Leonis along the same lines.

Nettlecombe was originally known as Netelcumbe and, not surprisingly, was a 'valley where the nettles grow'.

Returning back to the road I then walked along the Sticklepath, the name being from the Saxon 'staecle' meaning 'steep', before reaching Chidgley.

Chidgley together with Chedsey, Chedzey, Chedgly and Chedgey are 'proper' Somerset words with both individuals and villages having the name. Supposedly, the reason for the great variance in spelling stemmed from the seventeenth century poll tax where individuals were taxed, rather than property, and everyone had to have a distinguishing surname. Given the levels of literacy at the time astonishing variants of the original spellings cropped up.

As I headed downhill towards Roadwater, I crossed the 'Mineral Line' and passed an old crossing gate to my right.

Officially the 'West Somerset Mineral Railway', this was a standard gauge line running from ironstone mines in the Brendons to the port at Watchet. I would be visiting the start of this line on my journey back along the coast and I looked forward to finding our more about it.

DIRECTIONS

MONKSILVER TO ROADWATER

NOTE the Coleridge Way downloadable guide may be wrong here. From the Notley Arms head out of the top left hand corner of the car park and go through the churchyard. Exit the churchyard and head right along the road, turning left by the Old Rectory, entering a field and following the left hand field boundary. At the top of this hill, at a T junction turn right up Bird's Hill along a sunken path.

At the top of the hill and on reaching a road, continue straight ahead. After 300 yards there is a kissing gate to a view point and 100 yards further on the path continues right along a public bridleway through a five bar wooden gate. Cross the field at right angles to the road and head downhill on a woodland path, looking out for the blue squares on the trees. After half a mile, take the right hand fork marked bridleway to Roadwater.

At the road turn right downhill. Ignore a road on the left and 20 yards after this take the green lane on the left by Chidgley Hill Farm. At a crossing of paths take the public bridleway left to the Roadwater Valley Route. NOTE the path here is confusing. From the gate identify the beech hedge just to your right. There is no discernible path here, but head to the left hand side of the hedge and a path will appear in about 50 yards.

Enter Pitt Wood and head gently downhill. Continue through more open landscape before re-entering woods with a brief piece of open pasture by a stream. Continue straight ahead when the landscape opens up again, ignoring paths downhill to the left. At the road continue to head downhill to cross the Mineral Line into Roadwater.

ROADWATER, LUXBOROUGH AND A MIRACLE

On entering Roadwater there is a shop a hundred yards up on the right together with a Methodist chapel, built in 1907 by the Trevelyans of Nettlecombe as part of a strong temperance movement in the area. However, I turned left here along the road.

Roadwater, originally 'Rode on or by the water', followed the Washford River and supported a number of mills in the eighteenth and nineteenth centuries. It's a long, linear village, but I was soon out the other end as the scenery again opened up.

The pub, The Valiant Soldier dates from the eighteenth century with its roaring log fires and 'traditional' interior. Mike, the current landlord, made Ozy and I very welcome. I asked my normal question about whether the pub had a resident ghost or if any famous personages had stayed there and Mike said "sadly not". However, and nearly as an afterthought, he produced a visitors' book dating from 1935 that turned out to be a treasure trove of information about the movements of people in the decades both before and after the Second World War.

The first entry was a poem written in 1935...

Hiking along in a weary mood
Refreshment I found, both drink and food
(For the zider there was 'terrible gude')
At the Sign of the Valiant Soldier.

"Pray can you give me board and meat?"
I asked my host in accents sweet.
"For here I'll stop 'till I MUST retreat"
From the Sign of the Valiant Soldier.

Active Service at once gave he,
Kind attention that suited me.

And where'er I am, I'd much rather be
At the Sign of the Valiant Soldier   *Ima. I. Kerr*

Then on 12th July 1957...

If you can eat a 'Valiant Soldier' dinner,
And stretch your plate – like Oliver – for more.

If you can spend a solid evening drinking,
And not end flat out on your bedroom floor.

If you can say the beds are hard and lumpy,
Or leave the 'Soldier' feeling you've been "done".

Why, then you'll be a dissatisfied client,
And – what is more – you'll be the only one!

With apologies [to Rudyard Kipling], Keith and Pat Baldwin
(Liverpool)

I felt very comfortable at the Valiant Soldier, but with more miles to cover, I departed with memories of a bygone and slightly more polite age than today's Trip Advisor fuelled acerbity.

Outside the village I came across an old brick World War II pill box by Vale House. The box was originally camouflaged to look like a garden building with a pitched roof and painted windows and is technically a 'type 24 pillbox'. It would have held eight men and formed part of the North Somerset inland defence. Other Somerset pill boxes were camouflaged as bus shelters, signal boxes and seaside kiosks. The building was scheduled as a 'monument' in 2002.

I sat on the wall by the pill box and enjoyed wild strawberries from the hedgerow together with a couple of squares of Cadbury's before my next 'up' – Langridge Wood.

The wood is part of the Dunster Estate, in turn part of the Crown Estate and as I neared the top I looked out for the 'cist' marked on the OS map. In my ignorance I was looking for a well or 'cistern' which I assumed was from the Roman or Latin. How naive! Both the word 'cistern' and this 'cist' come from the Greek for 'box' and what I was looking for was a Bronze Age burial place.

Cists are often part of a more elaborate monument, perhaps a bigger cairn or barrow together with burial goods. This Bronze Age cist is one of only a handful found on Exmoor. The mound or cairn surrounding the grave was discovered when it was used for road material in 1820 and is part of a longer barrow. The cist is lined with slate slabs, and a five feet square top or cap stone. The body found inside was reburied in the churchyard at Treborough close by.

This monument reminded me of how much ancient history there is in the area and a quick look at the map shows barrows and tumulus dotted all over the place with the oddly named 'Naked Boy's Stone' just to the south of where I was standing. For those interested, the stone is either prehistoric or medieval marking an ancient trackway starting from the River Parrett near to where the Coleridge Way starts back in Nether Stowey.

Heading down to Pooltown and Kingsbridge I got rather lost both in the open fields and heading down into a farm. It looked suspiciously as if the waymarkers had been 'disappeared', but I found three farmers in Somerset farmers' mode, all leaning, arms crossed, on a gate watching the world go by. They soon put me right and pointed Ozy and me in the right direction mentioning, by way of a passing comment, that most people get lost around this part of the walk. Perhaps, it would be helpful then if they put some signs up rather than camouflaging them!

The farmers did, however, give me some good news though. The Royal Oak at Luxborough was open. So I practically skipped downhill to the pub in anticipation of a foaming pint of ale.

The pub's closed – not just closed but closed down. Damn and Blast! (Actually my exact words are unprintable).

The pub had been there since the fourteenth century and had changed little in all those years; with its original flagstone flooring, inglenook fireplace and open beams. However, I sat outside with a packet of crisps and a bottle of water dreaming of what that pint would have tasted like.

And then a miracle happened. Two men pulled up in a car and approached the front door. They informed me that they were working for the administrators and were keeping the pub open until new owners could be found. I asked, tentatively, whether they would serve me with a pint and they said "yes". There is nothing better than a pint anticipated, denied and then miraculously available I can assure you. And to show my appreciation, I had a second.

So with thanks, and a pint bought for the two exceedingly kind gentlemen, Ozy and I headed back to the path for the next leg of our journey.

The next destination would be the wide open expanse of Lype Common and up to the top of Lype Hill. The guide here was a little difficult to follow and it pays to keep an eye open for the quill markings on fence posts, some of which are starting to wear away or are covered in lichen. Therefore I was quite dependant on my map and walking in the right general direction. I can imagine that this would be quite a task in the snow or fog, especially if the Kennisham Hill transmitters were shrouded in mist.

The open scenery here was somewhat featureless with wire fencing penning in sheep. I could hear skylarks above us, but couldn't see them as they were way too high. It is these birds that were the reason why I had Ozy on a lead at this point. Under the open access rules, in place from March to July, ground nesting birds are protected from the marauding paws of clumsy Labradors like Ozy.

The Countryside and Rights of Way Act 2000, known as CRoW or the 'right to roam' (and *jus spatiandi et manendi* for you lovers of Latin meaning; a legal right of way, and enjoyment granted to the public, but only for the purposes of recreation or education) was implemented after pressure by walking groups, including the Ramblers' Association, to allow unfettered access to some of England and Wales' most beautiful upland and uncultivated landscapes. I'm therefore not unhappy to have Ozy on a lead if it allows me to wander to places off the beaten track.

This leads me onto another of my bugbears. Poo!

Yes, I know that it's sometimes inconvenient to have to pick up the little presents delivered by our canine companions and then carry them around but there is nothing worse than walking, especially near to civilization, and treading in something nasty. Worse still, are those people who bag up the mess then leave the bag on a tree, as if the poo fairy will come along and collect up the bags overnight!

However, where the event happens discretely in open countryside and there is no risk of domesticated animals eating the stuff then I'm happy to leave it as long as it doesn't bother anyone. And, on this note I think this is a lovely poem on the subject:

If your dog should do a plop, take a while and make a stop, just find a stick and flick it wide into the undergrowth at the side.

If your dog should do a do, you don't want it on your shoe, find a stick, pick a spot, flick into the bushes so it can rot.

If you dog should do a poo, this is what you should do, just find a stick and flick it wide into the undergrowth at the side.

If your dog should make a mess, there really is no need to stress, find a stick, pick a spot, flick into the bushes so it can rot.

(With permission from the Forestry Commission)

Rant over.

Now, where was I?

At the windswept top of Lype Hill I found a Bronze Age bowl barrow and trig point (423 metres). In fact there appeared to be three of these barrows in the area with the second nearest the trig point having a concrete lintel and padlocked door. I wondered if this had been used during the war as another pill box as the view from it would have been spectacular.

My route now took me downhill to descend to Wheddon Cross, my next overnight stop.

DIRECTIONS

ROADWATER TO LUXBOROUGH

Turn left along the main road (having come past the mineral line), passing the Valiant Soldier (PH) on the right. After 400 yards and just past the pill box, turn right along the road signposted to Luxborough. After a good ¼ mile ignore a sign to Treborough Wood (1) and continue along the road for 100 yards and take the steep footpath on the left signposted Treborough Lane 1½ miles. Towards the top of the hill pass the Langridge Wood Cist on the left and continue straight ahead to Higher Court Farm. At the end of the woods enter the field by the metal barn and head uphill. At the top of the field take the stile into a green lane and follow the contour of the hill by the right hand field boundary, navigating around any obstacles.

On reaching the road, immediately turn right through a farm gate and head diagonally left ahead aiming for the left of a row of trees, exiting at the top left of this field. In the next field follow the left hand field boundary and follow the footpath sign in the next field to the right and after 50 yards enter the next field which is habitually littered with old farm equipment. At the water trough head towards the farm barns ahead and right. NOTE this can be confusing at this point. Head through the farm gate and follow the Luxborough ¾ mile sign through a messy farmyard. Head to the right of a breezeblock and wooden cow shed and then right down a green lane. This can be churned up and you may have to take a parallel route in the field to your left.

Continue in the same direction in the open field soon entering a series of gated green lanes. On reaching a renovated cottage continue straight ahead, Kingsbridge ¼ mile. At the road by Spring Cottage turn right for the Royal Oak (PH) at Luxborough or left along to road to follow CW.

DIRECTIONS

LUXBOROUGH TO CUTCOMBE

From Spring Cottage continue along the road and at the junction take the right hand fork signposted to Dunster 5½ miles. Ignore path at Langham Farm Chargot Lodge, continue along the road. After 400 yards (100 yards past the house), turn left along the tarmac track, later through Newcombe Farm and then out the other side up a steep dirt track. At the top of the hill, at a T junction turn left along a green and rutted lane signposted to Lype Hill.

20 yards from the top of the hill, take a gate into a field on the right and after 10 yards turn right across the field signposted Cutcombe 2½ miles. NOTE Lype Common can be difficult to navigate. Initially keep the common boundary to the right. As you approach a fence head diagonally left to meet a gate about 30 yards in. The path cuts though this large field, but to avoid missing the next gate it is better to follow the left hand field fence. The large transmitter soon appears on your left. Go through a number of fields heading in a similar direction following the finger posts.

At the trig point again continue into the next field and into a last field, cross the road and cross diagonally left and also diagonally left across the field, exiting on the opposite side. Cross diagonally left again in the next field, through the gate and head right gently downhill passing through two gates. At the farm continue along the track straight ahead and then through the green gates. At the end of the green lane turn right and follow another green lane. Cross the road and continue in the same direction. At the road follow the signs to Cutcombe.

At Courtway House/South Cleeve/Church Cottages turn left nearly doubling back on yourself. At the corner at Little Slade and Rowan Cottages turn left down the road for the Rest and Be Thankful (PH) at Wheddon Cross or straight ahead for CW.

EXMOOR – SOMERSET INTO DEVON

And so Ozy and I came to the end of our second day's walking as we approached Cutcombe along a rather slippery track. The village name comes from the old English meaning Cuda's valley. Thereafter, William de Mohun of Dunster was granted the land after 1066.

Ozy and I diverted off the official route here to reach Wheddon Cross and to find our comfortable B&B for the night. This is Exmoor's highest village with stunning views of the highest point on the moor, Dunkery Beacon.

The pub at Wheddon Cross is the Rest and Be Thankful and is a 200 year old coaching inn originally catering for travellers on their way between Dunster and Dulverton. Ozy and I were well looked after here and soon got into conversation with the locals. I was told that the best time to visit the village is in February when 'Snowdrop Valley' comes to life.

In early spring the Avill Valley is blanketed with the small white flowers. However, these plants do not occur naturally in England and are not documented until mentioned in medieval manuscripts, written by the monks, calling them "snow-piercers". It is likely that Benedictine monks from Dunster Priory introduced the flowers to the valley some 800 years ago.

The flowers were probably grown to be sold by the monks at Candlemas (2nd February) - the feast of the purification of the Virgin Mary.

'The snowdrop, in purest white arraie, first rears her hedde on Candlemas daie'

Whilst there is no record of Coleridge or Wordsworth visiting the site I would like to think Wordsworths' *To a Snowdrop*' was inspired by the sight;

'Chaste Snowdrop, venturous harbinger of Spring,
And pensive monitor of fleeting years!'

And with thoughts of snow-white flowers on our minds Ozy and I walked back to our accommodation looking forward to our beds.

*****

Day Three was our shortest day and I'd arranged to meet two people who know a great deal about the area; Yvonne Gay who takes people up onto Exmoor to extoll the mental health benefits of walking in the hills and then later I would hook up with Chris Jelley, whose QR poems have kept me entertained throughout this walk. But first breakfast.

A full English breakfast is the only way to start a day's walking. A continental just doesn't even start to get you in the mood. Personally, I quite like Somerset Maugham's quote that "To eat well in England you should have breakfast three times a day."

Whilst we Brits are fully aware of what is expected of a 'full English' it seems that those visiting from abroad need some guidance in this aspect of English culture. The guidebook that was being read by our European cousins at the next table in our B&B took great pains to describe this culinary delight:

The traditional English breakfast, or 'full English' usually kicks off with a choice of cereals, followed by a plate of eggs, sausage, bacon, tomatoes, mushrooms – all of which may well be fried plus baked beans, toast (or sometimes fried bread) and tea or coffee. Travellers in northern England may also be offered black pudding, a type of sausage made from pork fat, onions, oatmeal and congealed blood.

My breakfast didn't come with congealed blood, nor was it the whisky and a cigar with which Churchill started his day, but it was good all the same.

So the first thing to do after a full English is to... 'walk it off'.

Ozy and I retraced our steps back to Cutcombe to re-join the path heading towards Raleigh Manor and the Avill Valley where the snowdrops can be seen in the early spring. As I walked down the drive to the Manor a strange looking tree caught my attention and on closer inspection I saw that it was a mobile telephone mast, well disguised, no doubt to appease the planning authorities.

As I entered Little Quarne Wood the scent of wild fungi and cut pine was in the air and the fragrance reminded me of being in the dense woodlands in Spain and I half expected to see wild boar crossing the path. The aroma of fungi appeared to come from the King Alfred's Cakes or Coal Fungus growing on a dead tree. These small round balls get their name from the story of King Alfred burning the cakes down on the Somerset Levels and the coal reference from the fact that they both look like coal and can be used as tinder.

From Little Quarne Wood I entered Blagdon Wood and from here I got my first glimpse of Dunkery through the trees. Whilst the weather was pleasant, the wind was soughing eerily in the breeze sending a quick shiver down my spine. Ozy didn't appear to care or notice.

Most of the morning had been walking downhill, but for every descent there is a corresponding incline and I now needed to climb to skirt round Dunkery Hill. I took a well-deserved rest under a perfectly shaped beech tree at the top where a horse fly bit me. Having never been previously bitten by one of these dreadful insects I had now amassed four bites in two days and was very pleased at having a well-stocked first aid kit with me, although my supply of anti-histamine cream was now running a bit low.

We were now as high as we were going to get on this walk and entered open scrub following the contour with the hill and beacon on our left. The moorland contained bell and ling heather along with the gorse which smelt faintly of coconut. As we descended I caught my first sight of Wootton Courtenay in the distance.

Ozy was worried about the Beast of Exmoor (not to be confused with the Beast of Bodmin) which is said to roam these moors, killing livestock and possibly black Labradors.

The first sightings of this elusive animal started in the 1970s and in 1983 a local farmer reported losing over a hundred sheep to the beast.

A few photographs have been taken, but as with any semi-mythical animal these tend to be from a long way away and usually without any other objects in view to give perspective, meaning the animal just looks like a black cat – which Ozy finds frightening anyway.

The most likely explanation is that the animal is a puma, panther or other exotic pet, beloved of seventies' rock stars, let loose after the

Dangerous Wild Animals Act of 1976 made it illegal to keep such creatures. In 2006 the British Big Cats Society confirmed that a skull found by a Devon farmer was, indeed, that of a puma.

In 1989 the West Somerset Free Press reported the washing up of a panther type animal at Blue Anchor. Disappointingly, this turned out to be a very exotic common grey seal.

Whatever it is, the Beast hasn't been seen for a number of years and even if two animals had bred the resulting offspring are unlikely to have survived for very long. In addition, DEFRA have stated that they do not believe that any giant cats are now living wild in England. Ozy was wary all the same, not having much trust in the government.

DIRECTIONS

CUTCOMBE TO BROCKWELL

From Little Slade and Rowan Cottages follow signs to Dunkery Beacon into the field downhill. Cross the road and take Raleigh Manor track opposite. Just past Watercombe House take the right hand track and drive. At the finger post peel off right downhill. Take the woodland track looking out for a signpost along the Drapers Way steeply on the left.

At the road cross to join the path to Dunkery Gate 2 miles. After ½ mile at the next finger post follow bridleway to Dunkery Beacon, sharp right. On reaching the river, turn left signposted to Dunkery Gate criss-crossing the stream. At a fingerpost signposted to Spangate 1, turn right crossing the stream once more. After 100 yards turn left and walk steeply uphill.

At the top of the hill by the beech tree turn right to follow the wall (the finger post says Brockwell on the other side!). The path becomes indistinct in places but continue to walk in a similar direction. Beware the path peeling off to the right and continue straight ahead to follow the Brockwell signage descending along a rock-strewn path.

At a signpost to Brockwell/Hole Cross/Spangate bear left downhill, crossing a stream before heading up again. Near the top the path forks, turn left at the wall. Continue to follow signs to Brockwell heading into the woods. Keep left here to reach a signpost to Webbers Post, also marked 'Solvitur Ambulando'.

SOLVITUR AMBULANDO

As I walked into the woods at Brockwell I met a sweeping beech hedge and a low waymark sign with the words '*Solvitur Ambulando*' (It is solved by walking) scrawled on it. The phrase is attributed to St. Augustine of Hippo who suggested that a problem can be solved by actually doing something rather than just thinking about the solution. Personally, I think it has a secondary meaning; that a knotty problem can be solved by doing something else, in this case walking, taking one's mind off the issue at hand and letting the solution pop into your head when you least expect it - and what better place to meet my next walking companion, Yvonne Gay, who is waiting for Ozy and me in the woods.

Yvonne is a coach and mentor and often takes her clients up into the wilds of Exmoor as part of her therapeutic counselling sessions. We were also joined by her enthusiastic dog, Bounce. So while I prepared to be enlightened, the two dogs ran manically around doing their best to disrupt our new found peace and serenity.

Yvonne told me that gentle exercise releases chemicals and hormones into the brain that make us feel good, boosting self-esteem, concentration and sleep quality as well as keeping us fit and looking and feeling healthier.

Taking a well-deserved break from the stress and speed of everyday life also improves an individual's feeling of self-worth and fosters confidence. It gives us more energy, a focus and a sense of having achieved something, even if the walk is a meandering one with no real destination. For those with depression or anxiety issues walking can help to relieve these as well as improving overall cognitive performance. All this from a stroll in the countryside!

Walking is free, easy, low impact, accessible and can be fitted into most days, even a very busy day in the office will benefit from a walk around the block to clear the mind, or perhaps concentrate the mind and help solve any knotty little problem – hence *solvitur ambulando*.

Of course not only is walking good for our mental health it also aids our physical well-being; reducing weight and burning calories, reducing death rates from heart disease, stroke, diabetes and combatting high blood pressure, cholesterol and helping back pain. It may also help prevent some cancers.

If you also add in the benefits of walking with a dog, not the two mad animals running all over the place in front of us, but nice sensible pets, then you have a recipe for a long and healthy life with pet owners over 65 having 30% fewer visits to their GP – but probably more to the vets!

I'd had a conversation with Ian Faris at the beginning of the walk about how far Coleridge would have walked each day. Ian had worked out that it would have been about 20 to 25 miles. Whilst this would have been quite an achievement, it was not so far-fetched and if a cart had passed by Coleridge would, no doubt, have hitched a lift. Supposedly, Coleridge walked to Bristol Library to change books, an 80 mile round trip, and he regularly walked to preach in Taunton at the Unitarian Chapel, 32 miles there and back, which he did in a day. This is all without good roads, street lighting or Gortex boots.

All this activity put my 51 miles over four days to shame and I got to thinking about how fit I was going to get during the walk.

At about two miles an hour I would be walking for 26 hours or so over the four days, being 96 hours in total. 32 of those hours would be spent sleeping burning about 50 calories an hour then there would be eating, sitting drinking in pubs and strolling to and from accommodation etc.

The hill walking, carrying a pack burnt the most calories per hour at about 550 or 14,300 in total. Therefore over my four day trek I calculated that I was burning 5,850 calories a day, about 3,000 more than a day sitting in the office and pottering about.

3,000 calories equates to a pound in weight or four pounds over four days. However, there were four cooked breakfasts (850 calories a piece), pints in sixteen pubs (180 calories a pint) and pub dinners ... and a cream tea.

Looks like this is not quite the health-kick I'd hoped for!

POEMS AND PONIES

Ozy and I left Yvonne and Bounce to walk back to their home in Wootton Courtenay and the two of us continued across the open moorland of Dunkery Hill.

We now followed the contour lines of Dunster Path, although, given its distance from Dunster itself I was not overly sure how it got its name. This should be Exmoor at its most wild but it had been tamed, cultivated and lived on for thousands of years with the cairns and barrows uphill to my left standing testament to this.

On the top of the hill stands Dunkery Beacon the highest point on Exmoor and also the highest point in southern England outside Dartmoor – Somerset boasts a lot of 'seconds'!

The area has been inhabited since the Bronze Age and is the site of two Iron Age hill forts. There is also evidence of a deserted medieval village or settlement and on the top are two of Exmoor's largest 'hows' - Joaney and Robin How. The word 'how' comes from the Norse for burial mound.

As usual, there is some debate as to where the word 'Dunkery' comes from. I prefer the Welsh origin of 'din' meaning hillfort and 'creic' meaning rock – Dincreic.

Very little has changed since the hill was part of Henry II's 'Royal Forest of Exmoor' and it's not hard to imagine the royal party in the distance hunting the prolific red deer.

In the summer months the hill is blanketed in a purple coating of heather (ling and bell) and the yellow of gorse. Today I could also see the native Exmoor Ponies dotted about on the landscape.

Supposedly these horses are rarer than the giant panda and have been given 'endangered' status by the Rare Breeds Survival Trust, although they are not, as far as I know, part of any international 'Pony Diplomacy' programme like their more cuddly oriental cousins.

The Exmoor pony is one of the 'cold-weather breeds' that have acclimatised and thrived on the frigid and barren slopes of many of the UK's more inhospitable areas. They have coarse oily hair, called a 'frost cap', 'snow chute,'" or 'ice tail' that deflects rain away from the nether regions to exit from the long hair on the back of the hind legs. Below these are fine insulating hairs acting as a duvet. Even their eyes have adapted to the weather with extra flesh called a 'toad eye'. The animals we see today are semi-feral and free roaming. Their colouring is imaginatively known as 'brown'.

It is believed that horses have been present in the UK for over 700,000 years and fossil remains go back 50,000 years on Exmoor. The modern version of the horse may date back to the Ice Age and they were certainly used by the Romans to pull carts carrying iron, tin and copper to nearby ports. As usual our first firm reference of their existence comes from the Domesday Book.

A somewhat more unsavoury event nearly wiped out the breed in the recent past when they were used as target practice in the Second World War when the area became an army training ground. They were also poached by city dwellers for food. However, soon after this they were actively bred and now there are over 800 Exmoor ponies worldwide.

Today the ponies help keep down the Exmoor trees and undergrowth.

To my left I could see the church tower of St Mary in Luccombe, built around 1300. The village name derives from either Lufa's valley or the 'valley where the counting was done'. What they were counting is a mystery. Looking further north I could see Porlock Bay which would be our destination for the night.

As the open landscape was replaced by trees I entered Horner Hill and Wood. At my feet I found more whortleberries, the wild bilberries that had accompanied me throughout my journey through the Quantocks and Brendons.

Also known as the European blueberry (or blaeberry, hurtleberry huckleberry, winberry and fraughan) these are petit pois sized berries and should I have been walking these paths hundreds of years ago, I would be picking these as I went along to give me energy for the trip. Like their larger American cousins they are considered to be a 'super-fruit' curing all manner of ailments including stomach disorders and diabetes as well as circulatory problems, diarrhoea and they help you see in the dark.

In the past the berries were harvested, not only for fruit, but as a clothing dye. The second Sunday in July was known as Whortleberry Sunday when whole villages would 'gwain to moor, pickin' urts' in a holiday atmosphere. They are, however, fiddly to pick and after an hour on the hills the harvest can be disappointingly small with just enough for a small pie or perhaps a couple of jars of jam.

The pickers even had a rhyme for the event:

> *The first I pick, I eat;*
> *The second I pick, I toss away;*
> *The third I pick, goes in my can.*

We soon reached Webbers Post and back to civilisation with cars parked in the National Park car park. From here the views were spectacular looking out west and a helpful orientation board explained the history of the area telling me that we were in the Holnicote Estate (pronounced 'honey cut') and that Webbers Post was an ideal location for the local hunt to gather to spot deer.

The woods around here are home to all sorts of wildlife including pied flycatchers, wood warblers, lesser spotted woodpeckers, redstarts, dippers, curlews, snipe, skylarks, kestrels and merlins, the UK's smallest bird of prey. Horner Wood also has fourteen out of the sixteen UK species of bat.

The post itself is an ancient meeting point and what better place to meet up with Chris Jelley and his dog Fable.

Chris was keen to take me to see the Jubilee Hut and we took the easy access path through the woods, admiring the wood sculptures along the way. Chris is the embodiment of his enthusiasm for accessible poetry for a modern audience. Never without his battered trilby and mad professor hair, he has embraced the digital age to get children interested in modern forms of poetry and writing.

I asked Chris if he thought that Twitter could be used as a medium for poetry. Chris was very much of the opinion that it was an ideal training ground for expressing concise ideas and quickly knocked me out a tweet:

The Jubilee Hut, with its bench dedicated to Alfred Vowles of Porlock,

---

Storywalks @storywalks
Finger posts poems mark the rhythm, Place and prose all QR code hidden #ColeridgeWay

---

a writer, photographer and conservationist, is also home to a plethora of QR codes – some a little damaged due to Exmoor pony vandalism and a Story Box, another of Chris' literary ventures. These are small blue 'cash boxes' containing an elastic bound notebook, pencil and sharpener.

Each of the books contains the start of a story by a 'guest author' and visitors are encouraged to write a paragraph to continue the yarn, perhaps with an illustration. As you can imagine some of these are good, other authors didn't quite get the concept and some naughty boys will always write or draw something rude.

I bade goodbye to Chris and made my way down through Horner Wood towards Porlock crossing His Honour's Path and Judge's Ride before an ice cream beckoned at the Horner Vale Tearoom. I had an English toffee and butterscotch, Ozy went for vanilla. My spoon didn't work properly. Ozy used his tongue!

We then crossed the medieval packhorse bridge and as we met the road took a short detour to meet up with Jane and John Tucker at West Luccombe Farm. The Tuckers breed Exmoor Horn sheep, an ancient breed particularly suited to the harsh Exmoor climate.

Jane took me into a lower field to help hand feed a lamb from a bottle. The mother looked on asserting her proprietary rights by stamping her right front foot and looking on lovingly. Jane explained that the sheep are purely grass fed on the moors and that the meat has a distinctive flavour as the lamb is matured for a minimum of seven days and mutton fourteen days. Whilst it is the meat that the animals are bred for now, in the past it was for their fine wool.

However, the breed is not particularly prolific and in order to increase numbers, an Exmoor ewe is mated with a Blueface Leicester ram, a breed that habitually produces twins. The Leicester is not a particularly robust breed, but when the genes mix the hardy Exmoor wins through and produces an 'Exmoor Mule'.

We left Jane to her hand feeding, it's a harsh and hard life farming in these hills, and re-joined the path heading into Porlock, past Granny's Ride (named as it is such a gentle slope) and then left into the town itself. Ozy was back on his lead so he didn't kill himself in the traffic and I searched for our B&B for the night.

DIRECTIONS

BROCKWELL TO PORLOCK

From the *Solvitur Ambulando* post head towards Webbers Post and keep following these signs.

On reaching a sandy car parking area cross this, the road and the central reservation to cross a second road into the next car park. Take the path about 30 yards in on the right (the lower path) and then follow the permitted bridleway and 'Horner' sign heading left along a forest path. Pass the Jubilee Hut and after a couple of hundred yards take the left fork downhill and keep to the main path. Cross His Honour's Path and at the Judge's Ride turn left downhill to Horner.

Pass by the tearooms and after 200 yards, turn left over the packhorse bridge. On meeting the road continue uphill and then take the road right signposted to Porlock. At the next SCC signpost, continue straight ahead. On reaching the Coach Road, turn left by Doverhay Cottage and follow your nose into the High Street.

THE PERSON FROM PORLOCK

Porlock made a brilliant overnight stop with its many pubs, restaurants and cafés, in fact we were spoilt for choice and decided to visit as many pubs as possible. Well, it'd been a hard day!

This part of the South West has always been a tourist destination and I remembered the town from forty years ago when I visited with my parents and brother, Gareth. I also have a vague memory that it used to rain every day!

However, I am not alone in this remembrance. Robert Southey wrote a not entirely complimentary poem about Porlock containing lines such as;

Porlock! I shall forget thee not,
Here by the unwelcome summer rain confined

and

Dull rhymes to pass the duller hours away.

Perhaps the tourist board could use these in their next advertising campaign!

Porlock has two 'centres'; the main village and a mile down the road the harbour area - Porlock Weir. The former is a vibrant little town and the weir a sleepy little port that has changed little over the centuries. I would be passing through the weir on my return trip.

After my refreshing pint at The Royal Oak and dropping off my rucksack and a very sleepy Ozy at our B&B I popped out to explore and what better way to get a feel for the place than visiting the local museum?

The Dovery Manor Museum is housed in a mid-fifteenth century manor house. This would have been one of the town's grandest properties, although looking at the will of the then owner, Walter Popham, the bequests appear to be somewhat moderate for a man of his standing; "To my nephew John Trotte, minister, my best coate. My daughter Sarah, wife of John Trotte, a ewe lamb."

After Walter died the house may well have been the 'dower house' to Court Place. Such properties were usually moderately large houses available for use by the widow of the estate-owner – known as the 'dowager'.

Local museums are often a treasure trove of social history with residents willingly passing on historical family heirlooms to be carefully looked after. For example, the items from the past two World Wars give an insight into the everyday lives of very normal people here in this far corner of Somerset.

However, one not so normal resident, invented equipment which changed the lives of millions of people. Here I'm talking about Stephen Hales, the Rector of Porlock in the early 1700s who invented the pie funnel – the piece of kitchen equipment inserted into a pastry pie to vent the steam from it! He also found time to conduct experiments on animals that led to the accurate measurement of blood pressure, albeit that this was a somewhat more intrusive procedure involving the insertion of a tube into the artery – so much more of an event than just putting a rubber cuff round the top of your arm and pumping it up a bit!

Next stop was the Porlock Visitors' Centre where I had arranged to meet Ruth Hyatt, one of the volunteers at the centre. I started my tour with the garden which contained the Coleridge Memorial Garden dedicated to Coleridge, Kubla Khan and the Ancient Mariner with its Gaudi-esque mosaic and ruined boat set amongst seashore pebbles.

Ruth welcomed me into the old school building, crammed full of information about the area. However, our conversation soon turned towards a unique project being trialled in the bay, the Porlock oyster and mussel farm.

Porlock oysters always had a reputation for quality and taste and when they were discovered in the area became a welcome source of protein for the population, rich and poor alike. When the railway to Minehead was built in 1874 the oysters were transported to London and were regarded as a great delicacy.

However by the end of the century the beds had been overfished by interlopers from the east of England and the industry ended.

In 2014 volunteers re-sited the oyster beds, placing bouchot mussel poles in the bay and reintroducing oysters from Morecambe Bay in Lancashire. The trial has been a great success with oysters likely to be on sale later in 2015. These oysters are rated as grade A and therefore do not need to be cleaned before being eaten. Once the commercial operation starts it will be the first community sustainable shellfish farm in England.

Of course, many people know Porlock because of its hill, in fact the A39 has its very own Wikipedia page.

The hill rises 1,300 feet or 400 metres in two miles with a one in four gradient and a hairpin bend or two. I remember holidays from Kent in the 1960s and 70s when Porlock Hill became a highlight of the trip with bets on whether our old Renault would be able to get up it. In fact when 'motor cars' first faced the hill a £50 prize was awarded for the first car to drive up the hill: won by Mr. S.F. Edge, a noted rally driver in 1900. The first motorbike made it in 1909 and the first charabanc drove up in 1916.

Due to the hill's steepness many a vehicle had to adapt its journey. Stagecoaches would ask the gentlemen to alight and help push the ladies up and the Ship Inn stabled a couple of horses to help exhausted stagecoach horses to climb to the top. These were known as 'cock horses' as in the nursery rhyme; *Ride a cock horse to Banbury Cross.*

Because of the sheer (in every sense of the word) difficulty in getting up the hill, a less steep toll road was constructed. Known as the New Road (even though the route had existed for a hundred years) it wasn't immediately popular, mainly because of the very few vehicles on the road, so it was mainly used for horses and donkeys. The first year's takings were £7.

However, the new road gained in popularity when more and more people had vehicles and wanted to explore the delights of Exmoor. This led to improvements to the route and its eventual metalling. Originally, the tolls were taken at the Ship Inn where a small boy would swing round the post of the porch, collect the toll and then run to open the gate. The current toll house was built in the 1920s.

Of all the stories concerning the hill, the most extraordinary is that of the Lynmouth lifeboat at the turn of the last century.

On 12th January 1899 a raging storm hit the Bristol Channel and the Forrest Hall, a 1,900 ton three-master with thirteen crew and five apprentices, was adrift and in imminent danger of being battered against the craggy rocks of the north Somerset coast. With little or no hope of bringing the ship under control the captain sent up distress flares and prayed for rescue.

The Watchet lifeboat was nearest but the storm was too fierce and it was unable to enter the water. The next nearest station was Lynmouth, further along the coast and they were asked to help, which of course they did – not just the crew, but the whole village, who turned out to help launch the lifeboat – the Louisa.

The boat was dragged to the Esplanade ready to launch but the storm was too ferocious and attempt after attempt failed.

The coxswain, Jack Crocombe, had an idea, "Why not launch from Porlock Weir?" The only problem was that the Weir was thirteen miles away and up over Exmoor.

Despite the near impossibility of the task, even in fine weather, the crew and around a hundred of the villagers decided to give it a go and horses and ropes were made ready for the journey. Within an hour after the distress call to Lynmouth the Louisa started her journey.

Whilst thirteen miles seems a significant distance to pull a ten ton boat and trailer, two additional obstacles were placed in the way – the fact that many of the paths and roads were too narrow for the boat and two 1,400 foot hills, Countisbury and Porlock.

The route was pitch dark, slippery and the storm continued to rage. A wheel came off the carriage and had to be replaced and the men sent out in advance to widen the narrowest stretches of the route were up against it.

At the Blue Ball Inn at the top of Countisbury Hill the men and horses were given refreshments but the task now seemed impossible and most of the villagers trudged, beaten and deflated, home. However, Jack, the crew and twenty men decided to push on.

The top of Exmoor was relatively easy – to start with, but they soon came across lanes that were just too narrow for the boat and carriage and impossible for the advance diggers to widen. The boat therefore had to be manhandled around the moor, avoiding the bogs that could so easily sink the boat and men.

And then came Porlock Hill, one in four, and treacherous, even in good weather.

The horses were taken to the rear of the boat and slowly and surely the Louisa was allowed to slide down the hill. The commotion caused by the event alerted the Porlock residents who came out to help, even demolishing part of a house to allow the boat to pass through the narrowest part of the village.

Finally the crew reached the coast and with the help of the people of Porlock launched the lifeboat.

The Forrest Hall was an hour's row away and the Louisa reached it and kept it in position until a couple of tugs were able to tow the ship to Barry, across in Wales.

Dinner that night was at the Top Ship, the sister pub of the one at the Weir. Here I sat below a painting of Coleridge and friends in 'Southey's Corner' contemplating the last sixteen miles of my walk tomorrow and visiting the spot where STC wrote Kubla Khan. I should have had 'potted laver', a seaweed mush and favourite of Coleridge and Southey, but I chose instead the fish pie in homage to my nearness to the coast.

The pub is one of the oldest in the country dating back to 1290, although a hostelry is thought to have stood on the spot before that date. At that time the pub would have been much closer to the sea which would have lapped up to where the visitor centre is now situated. Therefore, the pub has many a story of smuggling and illegal activities taking place.

The pub website says that customers would arrive at the pub by pony and tether them up outside. At the end of the evening bar staff would load the now, semi-conscious, drinkers on to the backs of their animals who knew the way home and would deliver their charges safely. However, on occasion rider and horse would be mismatched resulting in the wrong drunk being delivered.

The first stagecoach came to the inn in 1843 with the residents of Porlock flocking to see this new-fangled vehicle. It was at this time that the toll road was completed and the pub was used as the original toll house. The old mounting blocks can still be seen which were used to help riders mount their horses and climb on and off stagecoaches.

With the advent of cars, the old yard became a petrol station with a hand operated pump and, no doubt, helped many a driver stuck on one of Porlock Hill's hairpin bends.

During the late eighteenth century naval pressgangs visited the pub, plying fit young men with drink until they were so drunk that they could be marched off to join His Majesty's Royal Navy. And it was also here that Southey wrote his *Porlock* poem, the one about it raining all the time!

So with a clean plate and a very tired dog I finished off my pint and we made our way to our very welcome beds at the B&B.

THE ROAD TO XANADU

I woke up to the smell of frying bacon and, as I opened the window wide, the delightful aroma of freshly roasting coffee. This was from the Miles tea and coffee merchants just around the corner and with whom I had arranged a visit for after breakfast.

After another, very well presented, full English prepared by my hosts, Janet and Nigel, and a bowl of delightful kibble for Ozy (making my pack another 150 grams lighter) both of us were stiff but ready for our 16 miles into Lynton. However, before starting off we followed our noses and headed for DJ Miles Tea and Coffee merchants.

Securing Ozy outside in the courtyard, I donned a paper hairnet and met Paul March a director of Miles and their coffee expert. Paul took me into the roasting building which, as you can imagine, was hot, very noisy and smelt fantastic.

Paul explained that the coffee comes from a bean which are the seeds

of a fruit, a bit like a cherry. They were quite pale at this stage although recognisable as coffee beans. The storage area was full of sacks of beans each holding 60 or 70 kilos from just under 20 different countries including some very interesting beans from Northern Thailand called Doi Chaang. This coffee is now grown as a substitute for the drugs that used to be grown in the area and are fairer than 'Fairtrade' with all the money being ploughed back into the village where it is grown.

We then moved to the roaster which is rotating noisily where 24 kilos of fresh beans are tumbling in 200°C heat. Mitch is the head roaster and every 20 seconds or so he took a few beans out of the roaster, using a thin tube, 'sighting' the beans and comparing them against the last roast to ensure that they are the same colour. Mitch also smelt the beans and listened to the subtle changes in tone as the beans were cooked and tumbled.

When the desired colour had been reached, Mitch disgorged the beans onto a large circular cooling tray and a paddle and fan rapidly cooled down the beans stopping the cooking process. Again this was noisy but the aromas I was getting were delightful.

The next process was to grind the beans and package them. I put my head into one of the storage bins and inhaled the pungent hazelnutty perfume of these fresh Colombian beans. Paul explained that storage of the finished product is paramount and whilst coffee does not need to be kept in the fridge, it does need an airtight container to stop the coffee oxidising and the essential oils from evaporating.

And so after seeing the process from start to finish it's now time for me to taste the coffee in the shop. Over a mug of Mr Miles' Blend Paul tells me that the family have been roasting coffee and blending tea for three generations since 1888 and take a very traditional approach to the business. Having said that, Paul is very aware of market trends and the company adapts as required.

I'm pretty sure that I am not getting all the flavours and aromas that I should be from my coffee, but then again I hadn't had the decades of experience that Paul and his colleagues had. Oh and one last interesting fact; the tasters use an old sixpence to weigh out the teas to be tasted while coffee is tasted using the weight of an old penny.

So, with a bladder full of coffee I said goodbye to Paul and his team and Ozy and I set off from Porlock towards Lynmouth. This part of the walk is an extension of the original path which previously ended in Porlock. It adds a further fifteen miles or so to the route and most importantly takes the walker past Coleridge's overnight stop where he wrote '*Kubla Khan*'.

The walk started with Ozy and I skirting around the hills behind West Porlock and Porlock Weir that I had visited the day before and looking down to the dun coloured saltmarsh and equally dun coloured sea – the Bristol Channel can be a bit murky on occasion.

I then climbed through Worthy Wood which set the heart racing and was pleased to get to the bridleway at the top and then the road to Ash and Parsonage Farms where Coleridge's Kubla Khan was written.

Now, there is some debate as to when and where Kubla Khan was penned. When Coleridge got round to publishing the poem in 1816 (at the prompting of Lord Byron) he said in the preface that it was written in the summer of 1797, the year he moved to the area. However, Coleridge's grandson suggests it was penned in May 1798, nearly a year later.

The location is even more tricky. Coleridge had travelled to Lynton for a short holiday and found himself unwell with 'a dysentery' and in need of a bed for the night. A note found amongst various of Coleridge's papers states that the poem was written 'at a farm house between Porlock and Lynton, a quarter of a mile from Culbone Church'. I can imagine learned scholars drawing arcs with compasses to ascertain the exact location of the farm.

Both Ash and Parsonage Farms fall within the correct radius of the church but this assumes that Coleridge was accurate in his 'quarter of a mile', which, quite frankly, is unlikely given his often addled state of mind. Both farms claim the poem was written at their location, and who can blame them? And then there's Culbone Parsonage near to Ash Farm which 'reputedly' put Coleridge up overnight...

Because of his illness, Coleridge had been prescribed an 'anodyne' (painkiller) - two grains of opium, causing him to fall into three hours of a profound sleep. However, moments before nodding off he had been reading Samuel Purchas' 'Pilgrimage', a series of religious travel stories, and the words *'Here the Khan Kubla commanded a palace to be built, and a stately garden thereunto. And thus ten miles of fertile ground were enclosed with a wall.'*

As soon as Coleridge woke up he grabbed paper, pen and ink and scribbled down the half-dreamed poem.

The plan was to write a two to three hundred line epic. However, Coleridge was interrupted by the now famous 'person on business from Porlock' and by the time he got back to writing he had forgotten the rest of the poem and Kubla Khan was to remain a fragment of some 54 lines only.

So who was this 'person from Porlock'?

Some suggest that there was no such person and Coleridge made him (or her) up to excuse his lack of memory or inability to finish the poem.

In fact the 'person from Porlock' has now become a metaphor for writer's block. Others say that the PFP could have been Coleridge's pharmaceutical supplier. Whoever interrupted Coleridge, it has spawned numerous theories, stories and plays and we will never know.

The Xanadu story probably comes from the travels of Marco Polo who visited the location in about 1275 from where Purchas got his story. Xanadu actually exists and lies to the north of the Great Wall of China and is now a UNESCO World Heritage Centre.

The poem, like that of the Ancient Mariner, has spawned a number of later artistic works and in the last few decades; a film starring Gene Kelly and Olivia Newton-John, *Xanadu* (not a great success by any stretch of the imagination), *Xanadu* by the Electric Light Orchestra (*A place where nobody dared to go, the love that we came to know. They call it Xanadu.*), Frankie Goes to Hollywood *Welcome to the Pleasuredome*, *Xanadu* by the Canadian rock band Rush and *The Legend of Xanadu* by Dave Dee, Dozy, Beaky, Mick & Tich. Arthur C Clarke parodied the poem when he was co-scripting the film *2001*, '*For MGM did Kubrick, Stan, A stately astrodome decree*'.

Being no nearer to understanding where Kubla Khan was written or perhaps understanding the poem itself, I set off back along the path.

At this point it was possible to take a detour to Culbone Church to see STC's starting point. However, I would be passing this on the way back and decided to save this treat for later.

The Coleridge Way then follows the upper of the South West Coast Paths (we would be taking the lower path on the return journey). This path seemed to go on and on with little waymarking but we were soon directed southwards to cross the A39.

At this point we walked through the field to the right of the drive to Lilycombe House, built in 1912 and designed by Countess Lovelace and C.F.A. Voysey, an architect, furniture, textile and wallpaper designer who specialised in the Arts and Crafts style. The Countess was the daughter of Ada Lovelace of whom we will hear more later.

DIRECTIONS

PORLOCK TO OARE

From the Ship Inn (PH) take the road opposite (New Road). Just after the Porlock Manor Estate orientation board peel off right to Porlock Weir 1½ miles. At a crossing of paths dissected by a large coniferous tree keep ahead steeply up. At the top turn right through wooden barriers signposted to Porlock Weir (NOTE no CW signage).

Cross the stream at the bottom of the combe, past the wooden community hall and at the road turn left towards Worthy Wood and Yearnor Mill Bridge. This soon becomes a track. Halfway up the hill the path bends round to the left but the CW bears right signposted to Worthy Wood. Keep following signs to Yearnor where signposted. At a sharp left hand bend in Worthy Wood follow the blue bridleway sign right. At the T junction turn right along cycle route 51.

At the road turn left and head gently uphill signposted to Culbone Hill. At the next junction turn sharp right to Countisbury and Lynmouth. Pass Ash and Parsonage Farms. There are few Coleridge Way signs along this stretch but keep walking and trust your nose.

On reaching a green caravan continue straight ahead (although the Culbone Inn lies at the top of this lane). After 100 yards it is possible to detour to Culbone Church. Walk round and through Silcombe Farm and this stretch is also part of the South West Coastal Path. At the end of this lengthy stretch and on meeting a road, turn left signposted Oare 2 miles. Cross the A39 and follow the public footpath to Oare across the field then sharp right along the same field. Head to the left of a plantation of trees, over a substantial stile and head slightly diagonally right to find a track through the heather. Follow signs to Oare to reach Oare Bridge.

OARE AND THE DOONES

As we approached Oare Ozy stopped dead in his tracks and sniffed tentatively at the ground.

"Ozy" I called, knowing what I was likely to find and I was not wrong. Curled up tightly on the path was an adder, seemingly asleep. I pulled Ozy away, the adder still asleep or playing dead.

Adders, whilst poisonous, rarely attack and are not aggressive snakes. They tend to bite only when caught or trodden on or when a stupid Labrador sticks his nose at them! Supposedly, adders have the most highly developed venom injecting mechanism of all snakes, but no one has died for twenty years or so from a bite.

If you are bitten the NHS guidelines are as follows; don't panic, keep calm, try to remember the shape (long and snakelike!), size and colour of the snake and keep the bit that's been bitten as still as possible. Then seek medical help. Rather than panic, think you're going to die, find you have no mobile coverage, have no idea who you would phone if you did and then continue walking to the next village.

We left the adder peacefully basking in the warm sun and headed downhill towards Oare Church, the location of one of the most famous events in English fiction – the shooting of Lorna Doone.

Published in 1869 by R.D. Blackmore, Lorna Doone is a historical romance, and almost impossible to read (in my considered opinion). It's written in a 'phonological' style, replicating the characters' accents and mode of speech.

The story is half fact, half fiction, possibly based on the fatal shooting of Mary Whiddon in a church at Chagford in Devon.

The story goes something like this ...

John Ridd is the son of a farmer who was murdered in cold blood by one of a clan of brigands, known as the Doones, sometime in the seventeenth century. The Doones were a noble family but had turned to the dark side, like robber barons of old. In fact, just down the road is Robber's Bridge, taking its name from the fact that much of the area was bandit country in past centuries. The Doones specialised in robbing, murdering and kidnapping.

Despite this awful event and John's desire for revenge, John gets on with his life, looking after his mother and sisters. As time goes by John meets and falls in love with the beautiful Lorna Doone. Unfortunately, Lorna is the granddaughter of Sir Ensor Doone, head of the tribe. Not only that, Lorna is sort of betrothed to Carver Doone, the heir to the Doone Valley. Lorna isn't keen on marrying Carver.

When Sir Ensor dies and Lorna is likely to be forced to marry Carver, John plans Lorna's escape. However, John's relationship with Lorna is not without its difficulties as she is still a member of the hated Doone clan – a sort of Romeo and Juliet scenario.

Things then take on a more confusing turn when one of the Ridd family notices that the necklace worn by Lorna belonged to a Lady Dugal who was robbed and murdered by the Doones sometime before. During this attack a daughter survives and it becomes clear that Lorna is that daughter, heiress to a huge fortune. Lorna (now Dugal) now needs to travel to London to sort out legal affairs and the marriage between her and John is put in peril due to her now, elevated, status.

Oh, sorry, I forgot to mention that the necklace is then stolen.

An outside historical event further muddies the water when Charles II dies and his illegitimate son, the Duke of Monmouth, challenges Charles' brother for the throne. The Doones, seeing an opportunity to reclaim family lands in Scotland, side with Monmouth who, unfortunately, loses the Battle of Sedgemoor.

Keeping up? Good...

John Ridd, who has also been involved in the Monmouth Rebellion, is captured and taken to London where he is reunited with Lorna. John then goes on to save Lorna's great uncle from an attack, is pardoned, given a title and returns to Exmoor. Of course, he is now worthy of Lorna.

John then leads an attack on the Doones and kills them all save for Carver who escapes with the chap who has Lorna's necklace.

Lorna then returns to Exmoor, after something to do with Judge Jeffreys, to marry John, or would have, if Carver hadn't shot her through the window at Oare Church. Carver escapes but is pursued by John. There is then a bit of a scrap and Carver drowns in a bog.

Lorna doesn't die and she and John live happily ever after.

A whole industry has grown up around the Doone epic and thousands of tourists visit the church to see where the attempted murder took place. The church guide allows the visitor to reconstruct the event, pointing out that the church was shorter than it is now and amateur ballistics' experts can try to work out the angles of trajectory for the near fatal musket shot.

IT'S A STORY!

But still an enduring one if you can ever get past the second page when the completely incomprehensible dialogue begins; *'"Hyur a be, ees fai, Jan Ridd"'*.

Ozy and I continued onwards, past Malmsmead and then skirted around the contours passing a path to the County Gate. This is the boundary between Somerset and Devon on the A39. Looking at the map it is also clear that nine tenths of Exmoor is in Somerset, rather than the popular misconception that Exmoor is in Devon.

The gate is the start of plenty of walks being on the bus route and has a car park, information centre and loos. The Grade II listed building was a staging post for coaches on the turnpike road and, as with every building in the area, has a connection with smuggling. The 'gate' has long since disappeared, but the posts remain.

For some reason this part of the walk seemed longer than the map suggested. This may be because it had been a long time since breakfast or the fact that there seems to be an unrelenting number of ups and downs. This was despite the fact that the views here were fantastic down along the East Lyn (Doone) Valley. My next stop was to be Leaford and Brendon with its bird feeder on the village signpost.

Oh grant that we may always know
Vales like Brendon, where we go

To recovering what is real
And learn again to think and feel.

The pub at Brendon is just over the bridge, The Staghunters, on the edge of the River Lyn. This was a very friendly pub and I soon got into conversation with Simon, the owner.

Simon told us that the inn stood on the site of an old Cistercian abbey and was originally known as the Millside Abbey Tavern in the nineteenth century. The oldest part of the pub was used as a chapel from 1976 to 1990 and a local priest often held a Latin mass in 'the chapel' (meaning the pub).

As it was lunchtime I decided it was time for a bacon and egg bap and was tickled by the small noticeboard on the bar which announced; 'Today's soup is **not** tomato and basil'.

The next hostelry, The Rockford Inn, was just down the road, but to get to it I was going to have to retrace my steps to get back on track.

Through the trees I saw a brown dot in the sky, obviously a bird of prey. I would not have been able to identify the bird had it not have been for a friend of mine, Chris McCooey who, having previously walked this stretch with me, had identified the bird as a hobby. He also told me an interesting story...

In 1947, Peter Adolf (an unfortunate name for someone just after the Second World War) invented a table football game with cardboard cut-out players attached to a 'button' base and goalkeepers attached to rods in order to make saves. There was even a piece of chalk to mark out a pitch on an old army blanket – well it was just after the war.

Adolf wanted to name his new game 'the Hobby' and duly went down to the Trademarks' Registry to register it. However, the application was refused as the name was too generic. Adolf therefore had to come up with another name and being a keen ornithologist was aware that the Latin name for the hobby, the bird, was *falco subbuteo*. So he called the football game Subbuteo.

The Rockford Inn was reached by way of a wooden bridge and I enjoyed a pint of ale pulled straight from the cask while sitting outside with only the sound of the water gurgling below me to break the silence.

Fully refreshed I continued along the wooded path until arriving at Watersmeet, the confluence of the East Lyn River and Hoar Oak Water. I turned down the chance to try out the water sports that take place on the river and decided to try the tea rooms which have been serving teas to visitors since 1901.

After lunch at The Staghunters, I'm not sure that I needed any further refreshment, but the cream tea with whortleberry jam was just too tempting and I passed a very agreeable half an hour chomping on scones, drinking Earl Grey and watching the world go by.

It was then with some trepidation that I strode off as this would be the last few miles of my journey though Wester Wood and then into Lynmouth.

DIRECTIONS

OARE TO LYNMOUTH

From the bridge walk 100 yards before sliding off left along a farm track signposted Malmsmead 1 mile. On reaching the farm, head to the right of a wire fence and navigate through the messy fields continuing in a similar (Malmsmead) direction. At the end of the farm turn left, ignore the bridge and follow the river, signposted to Ashton Cleeve ½ mile and Brendon 2 miles.

At the white cottage take the permitted path to Brendon following the river. The path climbs steeply then descends to cross a wooden footbridge on the right. The path then meanders up and down the contours of the valley, occasionally steeply, for a mile and a half. On reaching a pasture, turn sharp left, eventually descending down steps.

At the road turn left and at the T junction right along the road by the bird feeders. Left across the bridge will take you to the Staghunters Inn (PH). The CW continues straight ahead past the packhorse bridge. After 100 yards, peel off left to Rockford and Watersmeet. At a gate pass through a farm (dogs on leads here) and follow the river to the Rockford Bridge (pub across the river).

Head now along the river aiming first for Watersmeet then Lynmouth ignoring signs for Countisbury. Pass the café at Watersmeet and head for Lynmouth 2 miles. At Lynmouth itself the CW signs disappear but walk towards the sea and the tower on the harbour. Turn left onto the Esplanade and the Visitors' Centre and end of the walk is on the left.

LYNTON, LYNMOUTH AND OZY'S CERTIFICATE

And so the Coleridge Way part of our journey was at an end and Ozy and I walked along the pavements into the town, past busy shops and cafés full of tourists, heading towards the Pavilion National Park Centre, the official end of the walk.

Finishing a long distance path is often quite depressing. Yes, there are often blisters and poor weather and the odd disappointment but the enduring memory is always of a sense of achievement and having completed a challenge.

Perhaps the most disappointing aspect is that no one usually knows that you have undertaken the walk and there is little to show for it, and this is where the Visitor Centre comes up trumps by producing a certificate of completion.

Ozy was the first dog to receive a certificate. I'm not sure he quite understood the enormity of this honour, but he did get a biscuit which he was very pleased with. Unfortunately, he was unable to sign his name in the book so I did it for him.

So what do you do to celebrate such a momentous event? Have a beer of course and I headed into the Rising Sun for a pint of Sharps.

But the day was far from over and I still had a great deal of exploring to do both of Lynmouth and it's bigger sister, just up the road, Lynton.

The Victorian spin doctors and advertising geniuses called Lynmouth 'Little Switzerland', probably because of it vertiginous gorge where the East and West Lyn rivers meet. Thomas Gainsborough, said it was "the most delightful place for a landscape painter this country can boast" when he honeymooned here and most of the romantic poets turned up at some time or another.

The steepness of the hill dividing the two towns had always been a concern. Originally the road between Lynton and Lynmouth was one in three and journeying down a perilous activity. In turn this affected economic growth and expansion. Packhorses and carts had to take goods up and down the hill including heavy items such as coal and lime. In addition, the tourist industry brought increasing numbers of visitors from Bristol and Swansea, arriving by paddle steamer.

An imaginative solution had to be found and in December 1881 a letter appeared in the local paper suggesting a tramway between the two towns powered by water from the Lyn.

A few years later a project was proposed to construct a pier and lift. This solved the problem of disembarking at Lynmouth, which was normally by small boat, and getting out of the small town.

However, both of these plans faltered if only because of the length of the railway needed and its less than one in two gradient. What was needed was a far more sophisticated braking and safety system, something that then current funicular lifts and railways hadn't previously required.

By 1888 the problem had been solved and patents for the braking and hydraulic system filed. For two years any residual logistical problems were resolved and the new cliff railway opened for passengers on Easter Monday in 1890.

Unfortunately, it is a rather darker event that most people remember about the town, that of the flood disaster in 1952. Flooding was not unknown and the Lyn had wreaked havoc on at least two previous occasions in 1607 and 1796.

In the mid-August of 1952 a summer storm caused by warm wet air being forced upwards and cooling rapidly, deposited nine inches of rain over a 24 hour period in the area. The ground over Exmoor was already saturated after days of rain and water cascaded off the moors into already full watercourses.

Upstream in the Lyn Valley the river had been temporarily dammed by fallen trees causing a huge backlog of water. When this dam broke a huge wave of water rushed towards Lynmouth.

Lynmouth itself had built a culvert to contain the river and to reclaim land for business use and very quickly this too had become choked with trees and boulders. The force of the water sent all of this material into the tiny town, destroying over a hundred buildings, all but three of the 31 bridges across the river and three dozen cars that were swept into the sea. 34 people died in the disaster with over 400 being made homeless.

There was some suggestion that the event was man-made and that the RAF had been experimenting with 'cloud seeding' in order to promote rainfall. This appears to be a case of not letting the facts get in the way of a good story and the theory has been dismissed by experts as preposterous as a Hercules dropping a bit of dry ice or silver iodide wouldn't have made any difference.

The chances of a similar event happening again are now unlikely as the river has been diverted around the town. A permanent free exhibition in the Flood Memorial Hall tells the story with photos and images of the buildings which were washed away.

However, the river and its forceful flow has had beneficial uses over the years and the Lynmouth Power Station started electrical generation in 1890.

Charles Geen, one of two pioneering brothers of HEP (hydro-electric power) formed the Devon Electric Light Co and prepared a plan to build a power station to light the streets of Lynton and Lynmouth.

Joseph Swan had developed the filament bulb (independently of Eddison) in 1878 and by the 1880s street lighting began to appear in London. Geen believed that lighting Lynton and Lynmouth would give them a competitive advantage over other holiday resorts and set about planning. What was really needed was a cheap source of energy to power these lights, and what better way than the HEP. The only problem, as with most rivers, was the unreliability of the flow. This was solved by building a reservoir to store the water, releasing it at times of peak demand. This was the first time this had ever been done.

The turbine building was disguised as a domestic property so as not to look dissimilar from the other properties in the town and Lynmouth became one of the first towns in Britain to be lit by electricity. Geen also built an arc lamp and placed it on the Rhenish Tower at the end of Lynmouth pier in 1899 to act as a beacon which could clearly be seen in Wales, some 20 miles away, creating the UK's first light pollution.

And it is with this in mind that Ozy and I hopped on the cliff railway up to Lynton where I had arranged to be collected by Seb Jay to see what Exmoor looked like in total darkness.

Ozy was not quite sure what to make of the train/lift but with his one pound ticket clamped securely in his teeth, he watched nervously as the carriage made its gradual ascent up the cliff face.

At the top we met Seb who took us deep into Exmoor for our 'dark skies' experience.

Exmoor boasts so little light pollution that the National Park applied for International Dark-Sky Reserve status, an award administered by the International Dark-Sky Association (IDA) and got it – and was the first in Europe to do so.

Ozy and I reached West Withy Farm, a small holiday complex run by Ian Mabbutt, and Ian and Seb were soon manhandling a telescope from the house into the garden.

The telescope, about the same shape as a toilet roll tube and the size of a kitchen swing-top bin, was soon set up. All we now needed was for the clouds to disappear…

The gods were obviously in a good mood and after five minutes or so the sky started to clear and the half-moon could be seen clearly. Seb trained the telescope's sights on the moon and there it was, in all its high resolution glory.

The image I saw was upside down, crystal clear and amazing. What always looks like a perfectly round sphere to the naked eye had ragged edges, those edges being huge mountain ranges sticking up from the horizon. Where the moon was in shadow, gigantic craters could be seen on the surface, and all this from a telescope no bigger than a kitchen bin.

As the sky became darker and clearer we swivelled the telescope towards Venus, the brightest 'star' in the sky. This earth-like body was 70 or so million miles away and surprisingly not round, having phases like the moon. Seb told me that it had a mass not dissimilar to that of the Earth, but there the similarities ended with a mainly carbon dioxide atmosphere and clouds of neat sulphuric acid raining down on the surface.

Our next port of call was Jupiter, the third brightest object in the night sky. This is our solar system's largest planet and a giant ball of gas. I could clearly see the giant red spot, although this was grey through the viewfinder and to the right of the view three perfectly aligned moons which I think Seb told me were Io, Europa, and Ganymede.

Now the sky was completely dark and we homed in on what looked like a completely empty area of sky. This was the Crab Nebula and through the telescope turned out to be an area of hundreds of stars and the site of a supernova which could have been seen from Earth in the eleventh century as it lit up the sky.

By this time I was pretty frozen and thanking Ian, got a lift back with Seb to Lynton, making our way to the Crown Hotel for a nightcap.

The pub was rather basic and a couple of guitarists were playing blues as part of an open mic session. One of the guitarists was Peter Mariosa. Peter was one of *The Dimensions* an early sixties group famous for the fact that Rod Stewart played with them before he was famous. The group disbanded in 1968. Of course, I was too young to remember them.

With the last chords hanging in the air Ozy and I made our way back to our accommodation for the night; happy, content, perhaps a little sore and achy, but filled with a real sense of achievement.

And so I laid on my hotel bed, Ozy dreaming next to me on the floor, probably of rabbits and swimming and dangerous snakes, and I dozed off thanking Mr Coleridge for enthusing me to start this epic journey.

ROCK STARS

I woke at six o'clock to a magnificent view of the sea from my bedroom window and, filled with early morning enthusiasm, I decided to take the optional route extension into the Valley of the Rocks before breakfast.

The town was eerily silent as Ozy and I stepped out into the roseate glow of another beautiful day and climbed up to Lynton, zigzagging and crossing the sleeping cliff railway. At the top, we took North Walk into woodland and then entered into open coastal scenery with breath-taking views.

The coast path was paved and easy, that was until we encountered other early risers, a trippe of Cheviot Hills goats, obviously about as far away from home as they could be. These animals were introduced in 1976, but goats have roamed these hills prior to the Domesday Book.

Whilst these are quite a tourist attraction, they have had a rather mixed history with the herd being destroyed in the mid-1800s after butting domestic sheep off the cliff-side onto the rocks and into the sea. However, this lot are more intent on trying to eat one of Chris Jelley's Story Boxes and I valiantly rescue the box from the jaws of a particularly tenacious billy.

Ozy, on the other hand, gives them a wide berth, having heard stories of animals being head-butted to their deaths.

The reason for the extension is that Coleridge and Wordsworth visited the valley in late 1797 and it was here that they decided to co-compose an epic poem to be called '*The Wanderings of Cain*' about Adam's son who murdered his brother Abel.

Robert Southey visited the spot in August 1799 recording that it was "covered with huge stones ... the very bones and skeletons of the earth; rock reeling upon rock, stone piled upon stone, a huge terrific mass".

However, today's visitors appear to be less impressed and looking at the Trip Advisor page for the location one reviewer said... "not a lot to see to be honest there was car park and think you had to pay" and another

"...there is not a lot there, just goats, rocks...". Oh the romance of the modern reviewer!

I enjoyed the rocks and the goats and swung round to the hut at Poets' Corner, sitting on the bench, out of the wind, just listening to the silence before strolling back into Lynton along the road and back down to Lynmouth for a hearty breakfast.

DIRECTIONS

VALLEY OF THE ROCKS EXTENSION

From the Visitors' Centre take the steps on the right signposted to Coast Path/Valley of the Rocks 1½ miles. Zigzag up the steep path, crossing the cliff railway. At the top by the North Cliff Hotel turn right and follow the road and then onto the coast path. Continue to Castle Rock. This is slightly different from the official guide but takes in more of the coastal path. At the car park/turning area, turn left to walk up the road and to the Poets' Hut. Then follow the road over the cattle grid up into Lynton, through the town and down along Castle Hill continuing steeply downhill (taking care where there are no pavements) returning to Lynmouth.

THE SOUTH WEST COAST PATH

With yet another full English inside me it was time to start the return trip along the South West Coast Path.

The South West Coast Path is currently the longest waymarked long-distance footpath in the UK and a National Trail, administered by Natural England. I say 'currently' because this will soon become part of the England Coast Path, itself a new National Trail. It is hoped that this will be open in 2020 and, according to the National Trail website, will be 'one' of the longest coastal walking routes in the world.

Now, I don't know about you, but I would have hoped that a government supported and sponsored website would have been able to tell me for certain whether it will be the longest coastal path in the world. However, a quick search of the internet suggests that this is a somewhat more complex question than it at first seems.

The new England Coast path will be 2,795 miles (4,500 km). Currently, the longest coastal path appears to be the Irish, Wild Atlantic Way, running for 1,553 miles from County Cork in the south to Donegal in the north. Nothing else appears to come close, all the more reason for the National Trails website to accurately state this fact I would say.

Currently, the South West Coastal Path is 630 miles (1,014 km), running from Minehead through Devon and Cornwall to Poole Harbour in Dorset. On completion, a walker will have climbed almost four times the height of Mount Everest.

The coast path was originally the route used by coastguards and excise officers on the watch for smugglers and, up until 1913, regularly patrolled by them. Today, you will mainly see leisure walkers and in 2012 8.6 million tourists walked at least part of the path, with those completing all 630 miles taking seven to eight weeks on average.

I would only be walking 20 miles of the path to Minehead and so set off with Ozy. Looking east, there is a magnificent view of the headland, towards Countisbury Hill. This is the same hill that the Louisa lifeboat had to be carried up and I passed a sea shelter which houses a mosaic commemorating the event. This is quite a climb and it was not difficult to imagine the enormity of the task undertaken in getting the lifeboat to the top of the hill.

Once at the top the views back to Lynmouth were worth a few minutes of my time, especially as I was gasping for breath. Down below me were, now, inaccessible bays and coves formerly a favourite of nude bathers due to the seclusion provided by the treacherous paths to them.

I was now at Countisbury with its pub and church. Countisbury gets its name from the Saxon meaning 'camp on the hill' and was the site of a battle between Odda's Saxon army and Danish invaders led by Hubba in 878. The Saxons won.

It was a tad too early to stop at the Blue Ball Inn, towards the top of the hill, which was a shame. The Blue Ball has been so called since the eighteenth century through to 1986 when it briefly became the Blue Boar Inn and then the Sandpiper Inn for some reason.

The name of the blue ball, and there is one in the Quantocks as well, comes from the fact that these coaching inns had a pole outside them with a blue ball affixed. When the ball was raised, this informed the coach driver that a passenger was ready to embark.

After a couple of miles of up, the path levelled off as I reached the Foreland at the top of Butter Hill. Here the Coast Path cuts off the corner at the Foreland, but it is possible to walk round the Point. Having said that the wind was blowing strongly from the west and the path narrow and scree-like so Ozy and I decided that discretion was the better part of valour and avoided it.

Whilst the Point route would have taken us to the Lynmouth Foreland Lighthouse, it is possible to visit this using the much safer access road on the east side.

The lighthouse was built in 1900 guiding vessels through the Bristol Channel and, although it is no longer manned (it was automated in 1994), the lighthouse keeper's cottage is now a National Trust holiday cottage.

The trudge up the lighthouse service road took me into Chubhill Wood and Glenthorne Cliffs and three miles of woodland walking.

Much of this path allowed only brief glimpses of the sea to my left but one feature stood out, Sir Robert's Chair, a striking outcrop of rock at the depressingly named 'Desolation Point'.

Desolate itself is half a mile up the hill and consists of a couple of buildings. Perhaps its only claim to fame is that it is the unique home to a native broadleaf deciduous tree, the Whitebeam (Sorbus 'Taxon D'), one of the rarest trees in the UK.

So, who was Sir Robert?

One of the Sir Roberts was the master of the staghounds in 1554, dying in Exeter Gaol from a fever after a 'peculiar shooting affray at Croscombe Barton, near Lynton'.

More interestingly, I had heard tell of another Sir Robert forever driving a flaming chariot up the steep sided cliffs of Glenthorne. So, what had this poor man done to incur the wrath of the powers that be to haunt the area for eternal damnation?

It appears that this is a case of the past catching up with a thoroughly nasty individual.

Legend has it that in the dim and distant past, at the old manor of Cosscombe, a tenant farmer was awakened by a knock at the door. On opening the door he was met with 'a soldier, fatigued after a long march', begging for shelter for the night. At first the farmer refused but after much cajoling, agreed to let the man rest for the night.

Sometime after midnight, 'a great noise was heard at the gates and it was soon evident that a party of men were endeavouring to effect a forced entrance'. The farmer was not a fighting man, but the soldier immediately set to defend the property and shot the leader of the gang, a large man mounted upon a white horse. This man was none other than the evil Sir Robert and it was his intention to rob the farmer of the rent for the property that was due that day. Not only that, the defaulting tenant would then have been thrown out of his property.

Now, you would have thought that wandering Exmoor would have been punishment enough, but the story takes on a far more fantastical direction. It appears that Sir Robert was then forced to travel around the county in the shape of a black dog 'sometimes on foot and sometimes in a flaming carriage drawn by four elephants'!

Black dogs and stampeding elephants were unsettling to the local residents and a priest was called in to exorcise the ghost, succeeding in encircling him and forcing him to undertake the task of tying up bundles of sand with a sand rope on the local shoreline - this Sisyphean-like task designed to keep such spirits out of mischief.

A thoroughly nasty family all round.

It was perhaps the elephants that had caused the cliff erosion and frequent diversions along the path which Ozy and I were obliged to take. The trek through the woods would have been monotonous had it not been for the frequent groves of rhododendrons lining the path. Unfortunately, Ozy and I were not there when they were at their best but I could imagine how lovely they would have looked had we been there in spring.

Whilst these plants are lovely to look at, they have a poor reputation and are often demonised as both Himalayan Balsam and Japanese Knotweed are.

Originally, the shrubs were brought to Britain by the Victorians but soon became a problem by taking over vast areas, killing off indigenous species, blocking sunlight, causing harm to fish and causing 'mad honey disease' in humans.

We soon reached a solitary house, which I presumed was the gatehouse for Glenthorne House. Although not on the coastal path itself Glenthorne House below me and to the north east had its own ghost story.

The house itself was built in 1829/30 as a mock Tudor, gothic mansion by the Reverend Walter Halliday. Halliday was the son of a naval surgeon and banker from a long-established Scottish family whose fortune had been made during the Napoleonic Wars. When Walter's older brother died, Walter left the Church to set up a country estate in the family's name.

Walter was a fan of the Romantic poets and, in particular, Coleridge and Wordsworth. This led him to this part of the country where he established the Glenthorne Estate. Unfortunately, Walter died without having children and through the machinations of ancient inheritance law the estate passed to his nephew who, in turn, invested his inheritance in the new Lynton and Barnstaple Railway in partnership with Sir George Newnes, the editor of Strand magazine.

Newnes was the original publisher of Sherlock Holmes stories and perhaps it was he who sowed the seed for many of Sir Arthur Conan Doyle's stories, including the Hound of the Baskervilles. Read on …

The property is now owned by Sir Christopher Ondaatje who is a Sri Lankan born Canadian/English businessman, philanthropist, adventurer, writer and bob-sledding Olympian who bought Glenthorne House in 1984. Some 20 years later, on a cold December's night, Ondaatje was sitting in the house writing his book on Leonard Woolf in Ceylon (now

Sri Lanka). Woolf was a political theorist, author and husband of author Virginia Woolf.

Whilst struggling with the manuscript, Ondaatje was visited by the ghost of the long dead Reverend Walter Halliday who he described as an 'old gentleman, well wrapped up in a scarf and nightgown'.

Halliday started a conversation with Ondaatje, "I see that you're writing a book about Ceylon" he said and Ondaatje said he was but was finding it difficult. "A friend of my favourite nephew also came from Ceylon." continued Halliday, and then went on to tell the following story.

The nephew's friend worked in Colombo and fell in love with an aristocratic Sinhalese girl, married her and brought her back to Glenthorne. However, the marriage was not happy and the man confided to Halliday that the union had never been consummated. The reason for failure to form normal marital relations was that the wife confessed that her ancestors were the offspring from the relationship between a human being and a cat and she had a morbid lycanthropic fear that if they made love, she would be transformed into a lion or a leopard. Soon after this the wife disappeared. The nephew's friend searched for his missing wife but all he could find was a broken window, scratch marks on the window sill and large cat-like tracks leading away into the woods.

So, maybe one of Sherlock Holme's greatest stories came from here and that the Beast of Exmoor mystery has been going for longer than anyone imagined.

My route continued past the house and into a secluded valley where I came across a small shrine known as the Sisters' Fountain. It was here that, as legend has it, Joseph of Arimathea brought his great-nephew, Jesus, some two thousand years ago.

Whilst, at first, it seems somewhat fanciful that Joseph of Arimathea would have come to Britain, he was a Phoenician tin trader and would have travelled to Cornwall in search of the commodity. He would therefore have known the south west coast of the country well.

On this occasion, if the legend is to be believed, Joseph, possibly on his way to Glastonbury, landed at Glenthorne with Jesus in search of water. Finding none, Joseph struck the ground with his staff and a spring appeared prompting the flowing of the holy water.

The story is said to have inspired William Blake's famous poem '*Jerusalem*', later set to music by Sir Hubert Parry in 1916:

And did those feet in ancient time
Walk upon England's mountains green?
And was the Holy Lamb of God
On England's pleasant pastures seen?

From the Glenthorne Plantation Ozy and I then entered the next stretch of woodland at Embelle Wood, home to Driftwood Dave, a twenty-first century self-styled Robinson Crusoe. Ozy and I didn't bump into him, but if you see a grey haired and bearded gentleman in a brown fedora, send our regards.

CULBONE – A LITTLE PLACE WITH A BIG HISTORY

Our next port of call was Culbone reached by way of a broad forest track which was mercifully downhill.

Culbone is small, just a few houses in the parish of Oare and inconveniently without a road. The woods around the village were once a source of quality oak, used for shipbuilding, and a major charcoal burning industry grew up in the area. There was also a large trippe (second use and so much better than herd or flock!) of feral goats in the woods up until about 1910 and their hides were traded at Porlock along with the charcoal.

Culbone was originally known as Kitnor from the Anglo Saxon for 'cave' and 'sea shore' and may well have been a Celtic religious site and, for such a small place, it has a great deal of history. For instance, in 1265 it housed a group of 40 people who were considered to be a nuisance to society; unbelievers, magicians and the mentally insane. It was used as a prisoner of war camp in the fourteenth century for French soldiers, a home for East Indians who had been taken prisoner by the British in India and a prison colony in 1720. In the Second World War an anti-aircraft battery was built to monitor any planes flying up the Bristol Channel.

The hamlet is usually reached by way of the path from Porlock and it was this route that Coleridge possibly took when he stayed in Culbone and wrote his 'dream' poem, *Kubla Khan*, as he makes reference to this being a quarter of a mile from his starting point.

The Saxon church of St Beuno at Culbone is said to be England's smallest complete parish church in regular use. Such claims, prefaced by the words 'is said to be', always ring alarm bells (no pun intended) and a little research suggests that this claim is not quite true. It appears that Bremilham Church in Wiltshire is smaller, in fact so small that only the organist and vicar can fit inside. However, this fact came from an article found in the *Daily Mail*, so read into that what you will.

Whether the church is a record breaker or not, it is miniscule being only 35 feet long and 12 feet wide and was built to serve the community of charcoal burners in the woods. The leper window in the north wall evidences the fact that the church gave aid to these poor unfortunates who were supposedly as numerous as the deer in the woods. The last leper died in 1622.

The church's spire is said to have been blown off Porlock Church in a storm and was carried to Culbone. God obviously works in mysterious ways!

Saint Beuno, pronounced 'Bayno', was Welsh and born in the late sixth century. Legend has it that he rescued St. Winifred from King Caradoc, one of the kings of Gwent and a member of Arthur's Round Table.

It appears that Caradoc fancied the chaste nun, Winifred, and whilst drunk attacked her, tearing off her clothes. In panic she fled to her uncle Beuno's church but Caradoc was quicker and in a fit of rage took out his sword and cut her head off.

Beuno found Winifred's decapitated body with Caradoc standing over her and, as he took in the scene, a spring sprang from the spot where she had fallen. The uncle cursed Caradoc and, as he did so, Caradoc's family started to bark like dogs, only being able to stop if they bathed in the newly created spring.

Beuno then picked up his niece's head and popped it back on her neck and Winifred was immediately restored to health, with just a small scar to show where her head had been chopped off. And you thought the Porlock spire story was far-fetched!

And so Ozy and I sat quietly in the churchyard, taking in the peace and serenity of the moment with just the chirping of a blackbird and the lazy buzzing of a bee to keep us company. However, the church had not always been quite so peaceful in the past with its own decapitation event. The old assize records show that in 1280 the church's chaplain struck Albert of Esshe (Ash) on the head with a hatchet, killing him instantly.

With so much legend and fantasy I was looking forward to a somewhat more grounded set of facts and I found these in the ruined remains of Ashley Combe House in Yearnor Wood. This was the home of Ada Lovelace.

Ada was born in 1815 and was the only legitimate child of the poet Lord Byron and his wife Anne Isabella. Ada was a mathematical genius, a trait encouraged by her mother who saw her logic and aptitude as an antidote to her father's 'mad, bad and dangerous to know' lifestyle. She is regarded as the world's first computer programmer, a hundred years ahead of her time, who was a friend to, and worked with, Charles Babbage on his mechanical computer, known as the Analytical Engine. She also produced the first algorithm or process intended to be carried out by a mechanical device.

Interestingly, Ada described her studies as 'poetical science', something that Coleridge himself may well have understood given his interest in all things scientific and his friendship with Humphry Davy. She foresaw that computers could have more uses than just calculating devices and unsurprisingly was acquainted with Andrew Crosse (he of the Frankenstein mites) and Michael Faraday who 'excited all [her] fun'!

Ada died early at the age of 36. Had she lived longer, then who knows what she would have achieved, as Alan Turing, of World War II Bletchley Park fame, was influenced by the genius of her work.

All that remains of the house are a few walls and tunnels, but in its day the property was grand, being significantly improved in 1835 with an exotic terraced garden in the Italian style. The house was ornate with clock towers, spiral staircases and hot houses to grow exotic fruit. What it didn't have, however, were any bathrooms and a bath house was built into the cliffs on the beach where Ada could bathe in private. The remains of the stairs down to the shore and also a small fireplace in the upper room are still visible.

The tunnels that Ozy and I walked through were probably designed to allow workmen and the hoi polloi to pass through the estate without being seen by the residents and so, out of sight of anyone posh, Ozy and I made our way down to Porlock Weir.

DIRECTIONS

LYNMOUTH TO PORLOCK WEIR

From the Visitors' Centre head into the town, crossing the footbridge towards Rock House to follow the coast. At the beach turn right and head uphill signposted Minehead 20 miles. Join the road briefly and then rejoin the path signposted to Porlock. Pass the Blue Ball Inn on the right and continue straight ahead following the broad mown path and just past the church follow the coast path around the headland rather than towards the aerial at the top.

On reaching the Foreland, the coastal path swings round to the right (signposted Coastal Path and Lighthouse) although it is possible to walk around the Foreland itself. However, this path is narrow and scree covered and can be difficult and dangerous in poor weather conditions. On reaching the lighthouse service road (it is possible to take a detour to the lighthouse here) continue right up the road. As the road hairpins to the right, continue straight ahead, signposted to Cosgate Hill 3 miles, to follow a track into the woods. Climb the stile and immediately take the steps on the right at Glenthorne Cliffs. Continue through the woods for a couple of miles following the distinct path.

After a couple of miles in the woods and on reaching a track turn right signposted to Culbone. Pass the house on the right and immediately after the gates, take a path heading diagonally left downhill signposted Culbone 4 miles. Just past Sister's Fountain turn left at the T junction. After a steep descent on the wide path, and on hitting a stream, cross the stream and take the narrower path straight ahead. Keep on this path and then track, all the way to Culbone Church.

Leave the church by the gate nearest the church, turn left and left again to join the track signposted to Porlock Weir 2 miles. At a Y junction the National Tail sign (at the time of writing) appears to be pointing right uphill. Ignore this and continue on the track, left downhill. Continue to zig zag downhill and then through tunnels before the final descent to the weir. At the Worthy Road toll booth, turn left along the road. After 400 yards take the left hand track signposted Porlock Weir 1 mile.

PORLOCK WEIR

Having experienced the delights of Porlock on the way out, it was now time to visit its little sister, Porlock Weir. This was a pretty harbour village and it was easy to imagine how this would have looked in centuries past.

There has been a harbour here since 1422 and stakes had been driven into the beach for centuries to catch salmon at high tide, together with the poles used to grow the famous Porlock oysters. In the autumn, drift nets were stretched out to sea to catch herring which were landed and sold to 'jouders' who were local wholesalers. The herring were locally salted and eaten over the winter months.

Today, whilst having a few boats beached higgledy piggledy behind the harbour gates, the village does not have the air of a thriving port, although it does have a certain charm.

There was a very informative orientation board across the dockyard bridge including the fact that Bill Pollard, a local fisherman, became the face of Wills' Capstan (full strength) Navy Cut cigarettes and tobacco, launching a thousand hacking coughs and oceans of phlegm.

However, it was not just the fishing industry that supported the local economy. A far more lucrative, if not clandestine, industry had grown up in the vicinity, that of smuggling.

By the mid seventeenth century smuggling had become endemic in Somerset, so much so that the Surveyor-General of Customs, William Culliforde, visited the county only to discover that most of the small ports traded in illegal goods, often aided by the local Justices turning a blind eye, or taking their cut.

Porlock, it seems, was no different although the local customs' man, Richard Davis, was doing his best and Culliforde's report of 13th June 1682 states, 'I went to visit Porlock, which is about four miles from Mynehead, where there is a very deep Bay and a good Harbour for small

Vessells... The (Preventive) officer, Richard Davis, is an active young fellow, hath hitherto been paid £5 per Annum. by incidents; he very well deserves £10 per Ann.'

By 1723 Porlock Weir was importing salt for curing fish, dickers of hides (sheep and calves' skins) and limestone for fertilizer. Many of the goods came from Wales and English wood and minerals were then exported back. It has been suggested that the items attracting tax; tobacco, wine and spirits, tea and sugar, were somewhat more loosely accounted for and records were not quite so accurate!

Why Somerset was such a smugglers' paradise is simple. Bristol was England's second largest port and with ships passing through the channel in their hundreds it was easy for a small vessel to meet up with a ship laden with goods from the Americas and the Indies and help to lighten the load. The contraband would then disappear into the wilds of the Quantocks and Exmoor, never to be seen again. The locals were therefore mostly drunk I should imagine!

The village was sleepy today although a few drinkers were sitting outside the Ship (known locally as the 'Bottom Ship'). Ozy and I joined them, to enjoy a peaceful and beautiful view out across the coast to Wales.

Next door to the pub is the Anchor Hotel, now part of the Miller's empire – a group of small hotels set up by the late Martin Miller.

Martin was the Richard Branson of the antiques world; an entrepreneur, writer of Miller's Antiques Price Guide, gin maker and latterly hotelier. So Ozy and I popped into the reception to sneak a peek at the cornucopia of antiques stuffed into the place. The interior assailed the senses with thousands of books and mismatched artefacts from around the world.

Whilst Ozy was keen on the bowl of sweets at reception, I was more interested in trying a glass of Miller's Gin. So we sat down, me on a well-padded armchair and Ozy on an old worn mat and while Ozy sniffed around at dead, stuffed things I took my first sip of a gin and tonic.

I was told that the gin contains juniper, coriander, angelica, liquorice root, cassia bark and Florentine iris and, of course, Icelandic spring water, being the softest and purest water on earth (allegedly). I could also taste the orange, lemon and lime peel. Perfect.

I could have sat there all afternoon, but I was keen to visit the Exmoor Natural History Society's premises which lay just at the end of the car park.

Ozy and I poked our heads round the door and Michael Hankin invited us in and told us that the Society records the flora and fauna of Exmoor, helping to preserve all that is natural on the moors, including the rare Exmoor Ponies. I found out that the area is also famous for some fauna long lost and that some three thousand years ago the area was home to a now extinct breed of cattle, the aurochs.

In 1996 a particularly heavy storm broke through the sea defences at Porlock Weir, flooding the surrounding area and creating a new salt marsh. The storm also exposed an area of silt and within this mud was found the pelvis, ribs and backbone of this ancient breed of domesticated cattle.

The animal in question was about ten years old when it died and would have been one of the last of its species in the UK, as the breed died out here in the Bronze Age. Being large, horned bison, these animals are the wild ancestor of today's modern cattle.

Porlock Weir was to be our overnight stay that night so we retired to The Ship for food and beer before a good night's sleep ready for the next stage of our journey.

SELWORTHY BEACON (AND AN OWL)

Today was to be a short day of about eight miles and so Ozy and I were going to take things easy.

We strolled along the beach and across the flooded salt marsh, picking up wild samphire to chew upon. Samphire is a strange plant and not something you see often in the shops.

Originally called 'sampiere', a corruption of the French word 'Saint Pierre' (Saint Peter), it is also known as 'sea asparagus' or 'sea pickle'. Now it's becoming one of those trendy vegetables originally given away free at fish shops but now a delicacy sold by the bunch in posh London markets.

The route took us past the memorial to the United States' airmen that perished when their long-range bomber crashed after clipping Bossington Hill in poor visibility in 1942, and it was towards this hill that Ozy and I were then headed.

Bossington itself is a quaint chocolate box village with colourful houses, thatched roofs and prominent chimney stacks. Most of the properties are owned by the National Trust as part of the Holnicote Estate, pronounced 'honey cut'. It was here that I had arranged to meet Cathy and Rod from the Exmoor Owl & Hawk Centre at West Lynch Farm.

The attractive farmhouse was built in or around 1456 on the site of an earlier manor house which dated back to the Saxons in 830. The manor was given to the Abbey of Athelney in or around 900 by King Alfred the Great. Of course, it was at Athelney (or the Isle of Athelney), out in the Somerset Levels, where Alfred first hid from and then went on to defeat the Danes at the Battle of Edington in May 878. It was also here that Alfred supposedly burnt the cakes he was supposed to be watching.

Now, I don't want to be a spoilsport, but the story is probably a myth. Firstly, if there was something to be burnt, it was probably loaves and secondly, the whole episode is probably a romantic explanation for the decision-making process that Alfred went through before deciding to fight back against the Vikings. I think today we would call it 'mindfulness'. Interestingly the Vikings also had a similar loaf/cake burning story involving the aptronymically named Ragnar Hairybreeks.

Talking about Hairybreeks, what I really wanted to know about were the owls and other birds of prey at the centre and Rod was happy to oblige.

Rod told me that he had 23 birds of prey, 17 of them being owls. The remainder were a tawny eagle, palm nut vulture, Harris hawk and buzzard, together with the three macaws. I was introduced to Thistle a beautiful barn owl who was quite happy to be stroked behind the ears.

These barn owls are superb hunters, with Thistle here being able to hear the heartbeat of a short-tailed vole at 40 metres. Thistle's eyes take up 75 per cent of the skull whereas with us humans it's 5 per cent and because of this they can see better in the pitch black of night than we can see at midday.

Owls and humans have a certain synergy and from very early on we were encouraging owls into buildings to help keep the rodent population down. Here at West Lynch Farm the Medieval threshing barn had a purpose-built barn owl window to let the birds in to keep a watchful eye over the grain.

Whilst I could have stroked Thistle all day, Ozy and I had a hill to climb and so we retraced our steps to head towards Hurlstone Point.

Hurlstone is, where legend has it, Saint Dubricius, the patron saint of Porlock, had a stone throwing contest with the Devil. Dubricius was the illegitimate son of Efrddyl, the daughter of King Peibio Clafrog of Ergyng. However, Dubricius nearly didn't make it when his grandfather threw his mother into the River Wye when he discovered she was pregnant.

Dubricius had sailed over to England with his chum, Saint Culbone, on a cloak. The Devil was not happy with two saints invading his territory and Dubricius challenged him to a trial of strength. This involved pulling a large rock from the surrounding cliff face and lobbing it along the coast. Unfortunately for Dubricius, his stone caught in his cloak (no doubt sodden from being used as a boat) and the stone dropped into the sea. It is this stone that can be seen just below the point at low tide.

The Devil then had a go and pulled out an even larger rock, throwing it inland where it landed in a cloud of brimstone at the top of Porlock Hill. This was a good two miles away and quite an achievement.

As Dubricius had messed up his first throw the Devil, magnanimously, allowed him a second go and Dubricius, stripping off the sleeves of his cloak, threw his stone a few yards further than the Devil. These stones can still be seen at the top of Porlock Hill and are known as the Whitestones.

Today, Hurlstone Point is marked by a ruined coastguard station which was used up until the end of the Second World War.

After a few miles of easy and flat walking the next challenge was Hurlstone Combe up to Bossington Hill and onto Selworthy Beacon.

The beacon itself is just off the route of the South West Coastal Path but worth the short detour as it just doesn't feel right to miss out the highest points – whatever the environmental reasons for diverting people away.

Bronze Age inhabitants used this highest point for religious ceremonies and as a burial ground. More recently, the spot was used as a lookout post, hence the beacon, and this would have been lit in the event of the Vikings, Welsh, French or Spanish invading, depending on which century you happened to be in.

These fires were quite sophisticated and depended on the level of danger. One fire meant that the enemy had been spotted, two that invasion was imminent and three, "bugger, they're here".

Due south of the beacon is the village of Selworthy itself. This is a pretty little place owned by the National Trust and built by Sir Thomas Acland as an archetypal English village with thatched, lime washed cottages in which the retired workers from the Holnicote Estate were housed.

Whilst Ozy and I didn't have time for refreshments, there is a lovely tea room there which is open during the summer months.

After our hard climb, the path to Minehead was mercifully flat. Perhaps this was why the area was used as a Second World War tank training ground, probably flattening any number of hugely important archaeological sites under their caterpillar treads.

As we approached North Hill and the downward approach to Minehead, there was the opportunity to take an alternative route to the coast via the Burgundy Chapel.

Now, I would only recommend undertaking this detour in good weather conditions as the path is both steep and slippery when it has been raining. However, as the weather had been kind we clambered down the hill in search of the chapel.

The building was a ruin, very small and precariously perched on the cliff edge. Little appears to be known about it although it is thought to be a votive chapel i.e. voluntarily built, perhaps as a show of thanks for escaping one of the disastrous invasions of Burgundy in France in the fifteenth century.

With the chapel ticked off our list, we headed off down into the bright lights of Minehead, by far the biggest conurbation of the entire walk.

DIRECTIONS

PORLOCK WEIR TO MINEHEAD

From the weir, head up the road. After 400 yards, take the steps on the left signposted Coastal Path and head right along the stony beach. After another 400 yards or so, and just after a lonely oak tree, head inland signposted Bossington 2 miles. The path is well marked (although ignore a walkers' and stock gate you come across on the path). After approximately 1.5 miles into the walk, pass by the memorial to the crashed Liberator Bomber and cross the bridge and follow the mown path through Sparkhayes Marsh again following signs to Bossington.

On reaching Bossington walk through the village. At the village hall and car park, turn left (no signpost) down the drive to the ford and cross the river by the bridge, turning left into the woods and following the river. Start an uphill section to Hurlstone Point. At the marker, take a short detour up to the Point. Return by taking the left hand path (the right leads back to the marker) and at the first crossing of paths, turn left steeply uphill. Towards the top head towards Selworthy Beacon (rather than the coastal path).

DIRECTIONS

PORLOCK WEIR TO MINEHEAD CONTINUED

From the beacon and trig point, retrace your steps for 50 yards and take a track on the right heading downhill. After 100 yards, turn right to rejoin the coastal path. On meeting the end of tarmacked road keep straight ahead on the bridleway. As the field opens up, go through a gate at the Holnicote Estate sign and continue ahead following the National Trail arrow. At a car park and crossing of paths head downhill signposted to Minehead Harbour. After 100 yards the footpath turns right but straight ahead is the Burgundy Chapel. Here there are two alternatives.

EITHER you can follow the Coast Path route by turning right and following the path, then track, into woodland. At a gate (stating 'please shut the gate – ENP) and a crossing of paths, IGNORE the track straight ahead signposted Minehead 1.5 miles and take the path diagonally left behind you also to Minehead but 1.75 miles and follow this down through the woods, turning right at the bottom of the steps. After 400 yards, fork off left downhill as the road goes up hill and continue until reaching a park. At the road continue straight ahead, passing The Old Ship Aground pub, until reaching the official start of the South West Coast Path with the giant map sculpture.

OR visiting the Burgundy Chapel by taking the steep and narrow track downhill. This can be very slippery when wet underfoot. At a right hand turn by a bench, continue downhill. The chapel is accessed by steps on the right. Returning to the track, turn left following a path through the woods. At Greenaleigh Point the original path has slipped so you will need to follow any diversions. On reaching two houses pass through their drive and on meeting steps on the right, continue ahead. This is now the coastal path again. Follow this semi tarmacked path for 400 yards and then fork off left downhill as the road goes up hill and continue until reaching a park. At the road continue straight ahead, passing the pub (The Old Ship Aground), until reaching the official start of the South West Coast Path with the giant map sculpture.

MINEHEAD - BOATS, TRAINS AND SATELLITES

Ask anyone about Minehead and they will immediately say "Butlins", and, as Ozy and I headed into the town, the white canopied roof of the holiday camp came into, and stayed in, view. However, Minehead would, I hoped, offer far more than seaside, kiss me quick hats and ice cream and the two of us headed towards the main street.

Minehead comes from the old English word for the North Hill, 'Myned' which dominates the town, and has been populated since ancient times. Like all of these coastal towns along the Bristol Channel it has been subject to invasion with the Danes having a go in the ninth century, the Saxons under Lady Godiva's son in 1087 (when the population was a massive 69) and the Welsh in 1265.

Minehead was bought by Lady Elizabeth Luttrell in the 1400's for 10,000 marks. The Mark was not an actual coin but used for accounting purposes and each mark was worth 13 shillings and 4 pence. Therefore, the price of Minehead then was about £5,500 or three to four million pounds today.

My first thoughts, when looking at the sea-front houses, was that the front doors all appeared to be at the side of the properties, giving me the impression that the elements could be harsh on this stretch of the coast. But today was fair and calm as I walked into town.

The town harbour was on my left and on the harbour wall a series of seven bronze coloured plaques depicting the rich and varied history of the harbour designed by Sue Webber could be seen.

There was a small port here by 1380, but it was the Luttrells who improved the harbour, firstly in 1420 and then provided the town with a stone harbour and pier, which was completed in 1616.

In Elizabethan times the town had its own Port Officer and traded internationally with Wales, Ireland and even as far as La Rochelle in France.

Trade continued to grow and by the beginning of the eighteenth century forty vessels were based there. Then in the early nineteenth century ships travelled further abroad to Virginia in the United States and the West Indies. However, in 1834 the port lost its jurisdiction to Bridgwater and so started the slow decline of commercial trade with pleasure steamers taking their place.

The pier was demolished in the Second World War as it obstructed the view from the gun battery on the quay head. This stopped the steamers until the battery was demolished and cleared in 1951.

There were no steamers today and a few lone fishing boats bobbed about giving the harbour a lazy air.

I passed the Tea at the Quay café which was formerly the Mermaid and one of the oldest business premises in the town. It was here in 1634 that Old Mother Leakey lived and became known as the Whistling Ghost, notorious for 'whistling up a storm' whenever one of her son's ships neared port. This became such a problem that in 1636 the Bishop of Bath and Wells presided over a Royal Commission to inquire into the matter. Unfortunately, the commission's finding were inconclusive and, over time, the whistling faded away.

After a hundred or so yards, I passed the modern statue depicting the start of the South West Coastal Path; two colossal hands holding a map and the photographic focal point of probably every one starting this long-distance path. It is, perhaps, fitting that the path starts here as Minehead Harbour was also the departure point for pilgrims going to Santiago de Compostella in northern Spain in the 1800s.

The Hobby Horse on the right, just before the high street, had an air of faded glory and was named after yet another quirky local custom. During the first three days of May a brightly coloured cloth 'hobby horse' is traipsed around the streets of Minehead. This custom goes back to the Middle Ages and may even have been used to frighten off the Danes prior to that.

Today the horse, named for some obscure reason, 'the Sailor's Horse', looks very much like a ship and this modern version first appeared in 1830. There have been other pretenders to the hobby horse crown with a Dunster Horse in the 1920s, an Alcombe Horse in the 1930s and the Town Horse in the 1970s. Therefore, Minehead is, perhaps, not the one-horse town that I imagined it to be!

My next stop was the Beach Hotel, immediately opposite the West Somerset Railway terminus. I had two reasons to visit; firstly, because the visitors' centre and town museum are situated there and secondly, I had arranged to meet Dave Jackson, the General Manager of the hotel.

The building is an imposing white and grey painted Victorian building, yet with a contemporary look, something that carries on beyond the bricks and mortar of the exterior.

As a visitors' centre, it is worth a look, even if it is just to orientate yourself and check out the local history and pick up a souvenir of the town. However, in a room behind the counter is the museum full of artefacts from the surrounding area with plenty of reading material on the walls. I was intrigued by a number of small coins in a display case which were produced by the town. It transpires that in the seventeenth century there was no national supply of small change and therefore towns produced their own halfpennies and farthings. These had little or no value outside the local community and were not legal tender. An explanation for the lack of small coinage was that King Charles I considered it beneath his dignity to issue any coin in a metal other than silver and the silver farthing was just too small to produce.

Coleridge himself would have experienced a similar issue in 1797 when new coinage came into use for a not dissimilar reason.

In the eighteenth century coinage had a base metal value, coins would be silver or gold and actually worth something, rather than just a token. However, in the years approaching 1797 counterfeiting was rampant, coins were wearing out and small denomination change was becoming scarce. Therefore, two new copper coins came into general circulation and were nicknamed 'cartwheels'.

Because the value of the coin was represented in the value of the metal it contained they were huge. The penny was one ounce and the tuppence, two, the latter being 1.6 inches or 41cm. And one last fact; they were the first coins minted on a steam-driven machine.

After half an hour of reading the detailed information boards in the museum and Ozy having his picture taken with one of the volunteer curators, it was time to scrounge a coffee next door in the hotel.

Dave Jackson, the hipster-looking Director of Operations for YMCA Somerset Coast, had generously set aside time to have a chat.

Dave explained to me that the Beach Hotel is a YMCA project running a contemporary hotel and innovative restaurant employing apprentices and trainees from, what were often, difficult backgrounds or starts in life. The hotel runs as a non-profit organisation with every penny received being ploughed back in this project and others like it. In fact, it is the only such YMCA set-up in Europe and only three other similar enterprises exist in the world: Singapore, Hong Kong and Boston (US).

The hotel was originally built in 1874 in conjunction with the railway and was, unsurprisingly, supposed to be called the Railway Hotel, however, on the day it opened it called itself the Beach Hotel and the name stuck.

The hotel primarily catered for families and an aspiring Victorian and Edwardian middle class with suites of rooms being taken, not just for the family but also maids and other servants. In the 1950s the hotel belonged to the Forte group, still providing a top-notch service until the sixties and seventies when cheap foreign travel started the demise of the traditional seaside holiday and The Beach started to welcome coach parties of pensioners. From then on, the property became more and more dilapidated until it was purchased by the YMCA.

Today the hotel is an award-winning establishment with top class food and accommodation together with a social conscience – and it's also dog (and muddy dog) friendly, which made Ozy very happy.

It was with regret that I had to leave my proper coffee and freshly baked flapjacks and I headed into the centre of the town.

The main street, at right angles to the sea, contained a mixture of tourist shops, bars, restaurants and familiar chain stores and was the first, and last, conurbation along the route where I could stock up on anything needed. However, none of the buildings was over a couple of hundred years old due to a devastating fire which took place in 1791.

With houses made of wood and thatched roofs, fires were an inevitable fact of life and a candle, accidently knocked over, could start a conflagration that was difficult to contain. The Minehead fire had a more exotic beginning as a report at the time detailed:

'*Last Tuesday noon, Edward May, a miller of this place, was trying an experiment by burning a tar barrel, when the wind being very high, the fire communicated to a large stack of furze that stood in his yard, which instantly got into a blaze and spread with the greatest rapidity into the adjoining dwellings, so that before the next morning upwards of seventy-two houses, comprising almost the whole of the Middle Town, were reduced to ashes ... One life only was lost, that of Mr.D.Price, a poor maniac, who, being confined was, in the hurry and confusion, forgotten, till too late.*'

Minehead was to be Ozy and my overnight stop and we settled down for a late afternoon nap in our B&B before experiencing the nightlife the town had to offer.

Now, up until this point in our journey it had been possible to visit (or at least look in) every pub that we had come across (apart from the one non-dog friendly establishment at the beginning of the route). However, Minehead had far too many pubs and bars to make this possible, so a choice had to be made.

Seaside town pubs can often be disappointing. Many are huge cavernous affairs, catering for large groups of lager swilling punters or 'family pubs' with small, loud children running around clutching bottles of pop with straws sticking out of the top. To be fair, Minehead had few of these and I had a list of real ale establishments to try.

Had I been here a few hundred years ago, I could have visited The Key, The Lambe, The Kings Armes '*which is a good house and stables built on the wharfe gainst the sea*', The Newe Inn, and The Crooked Fish. Even up until recent times I could have had a pint in the Streaky Bacon House, so called because it was painted pink and white but, alas, this too had been knocked down.

However, on the outskirts of the town was a real ale haven, a hotel bar, The Kildare Lodge. I was going to say this pub looked a little dated, but that is not a criticism, as it had the right feel of an independent town hotel and the range of four beers was a bonus and a CAMRA favourite.

I had crossed out those pubs which did not allow Ozy, including the first Wetherspoons of my trip, and those in the town centre as being a little too commercial and headed back towards the sea front.

The Quay was bright and airy and had a good range of local ales and was a worthwhile stop and then The Old Ship Aground was our dinner and final stop. This pub was built in 1911 and originally The Pier Hotel, accommodating guests from the paddle steamers which then docked at the Old Pier.

And so with stomachs full and a final stroll along the, now silent sea front, Ozy and I made our way back to our guesthouse to fall into a deep dreamless sleep.

*****

During my early morning stroll to restart the trail, I walked past a rather splendid row of houses, one of which was the birthplace of Arthur C Clarke.

Arthur Charles Clarke was one of the UK's most famous science fiction writers, penning *2001: A Space Odyssey* in 1968, made into the iconic film by Stanley Kubrick. However, Clarke was much more than an author and in 1934, while still a teenager, he joined the British Interplanetary Society and a decade later outlined a global satellite communication system. This led him to envision geostationary communications satellites, the ability to broadcast television around the world and a *'personal transceiver, so small and compact that every man carries one [and] the time will come when we will be able to call a person anywhere on Earth merely by dialling a number'*. In turn, such a device would allow for global positioning so that *'no one need ever again be lost.'* – and here I was using a map and compass!

It seems that my low-tech approach was endorsed by the South West Coastal Path as I again reached the sculpture of two large hands holding an unfolding map. This was designed by Sarah Ward in 2001, who was studying at the West Somerset Community College at the time. And so I was back on track, but only for a short while as I was just about to take a very different track and met Paul Conibeare, the General Manager at the West Somerset Railway (WSR).

Paul produced a large mug of tea and we sat in the station-master's office to talk trains.

In 1845, proposals were discussed to build a line from Watchet to Bridport on the south coast. The main purpose of this route was to alleviate the need for ships to take the circuitous route around the coast of Cornwall. Much debate took place over the proposed route of the railway and Isambard Kingdom Brunel favoured a line from Bridgwater with a long tunnel under the Quantocks (Brunel liked tunnels). However, the Taunton route won out. The line opened in 1862 between Taunton and Watchet, and was extended to Minehead in 1874.

Whilst the carriage of goods from the south to the north coast was the original intention of the line, perhaps of most importance was the opening of Butlins holiday camp in Minehead attracting up to 30,000 holidaymakers a year in the early 1960s. However, even this number of passengers was not sufficient to escape the interest of the Beeching cuts and the line closed in 1971, albeit some considerable time after the 1963 recommendations. The reason? They were waiting for a replacement bus service to be put in place! It's now somewhat ironic that the bus service is now under threat and the railway is the only mode of public transport going to places like Blue Anchor.

The WSR opened as a heritage railway in March 1976 and is the longest standard gauge heritage railway in the UK at just under 23 miles long, running both steam and diesel trains.

The railway runs with a team of fifty staff and a thousand volunteers and is one of West Somerset's larger employers, contributing about ten million pounds to the local economy. The WSR carries about 200,000 visitors a year

Up until recently the railway station at Minehead also saw an annual CAMRA (Campaign for Real Ale) beer festival each September. At this event, the platform was narrowed by the building of a large bar, visitors were plied with copious amounts of local ale and then had steam trains driven at them. Whoever manged to get this past the health and safety jobsworths deserves a medal.

I thanked Paul for his time and the tea and walked up and down the platform taking in the sounds and smells of yesteryear, before returning to the path again.

On my right was the Queen's Hall, now a pub, but originally a theatre seeing such greats as Anna Pavlova and her ballet company perform there. It was also the venue for Minehead's first 'talkies' in the 1930s.

Further up the seafront was Butlins with its 'big top' style roof which can be seen for miles around. The site was chosen originally because of its flatness, proximity to the town and excellent rail links – little did they know of Dr Beeching's plans.

Opened in 1962, the holiday camp experience has changed and the site is now less Hi-De-Hi! and more Somerset Riviera. However, as Ozy wasn't allowed in we had to give Butlins a miss.

I waved goodbye to Minehead and after walking along the edge of the golf course I was back on the shingle of the coast and could see my next stop, Dunster Beach.

DUNSTER AND ITS CASTLE

A row of pretty, coloured beach huts greeted Ozy and me at Dunster Beach although the shop and kiosk were closed for the season.

The beach is at the end of the River Avill and used to have a well used harbour known as Dunster Haven. It was from here that wool and cloth were exported, although this trade ceased when the river started to silt up in the seventeenth century.

As today was to be another short day, Ozy and I had plenty of time to head the mile up into the village of Dunster itself.

Dunster and the surrounding area has been inhabited since the Iron Age and the village is mentioned in the Domesday Book. The name possibly comes from 'Dunn' a Saxon noble who held land nearby and the Saxon name for a rocky hill, 'torre'.

The most prominent building in the High Street itself is the Yarn Market, an octagonal building built in the early seventeenth century, although there had been a thriving wool and clothing trade since the Middle Ages. The Luttrell family erected the building to promote the village as a prominent market town, especially as the shoreline was retreating and the nearest harbour silting up. However, wherever you look the eye is drawn to the castle on the hill above the village.

There has been a castle here prior to 1086 and the Normans built a timber castle here sometime in the eleventh century to subjugate us Brits. This was replaced by a stone affair by the beginning of the twelfth century and survived a siege during the 'Anarchy'.

The Anarchy was the period between 1135 and 1154 when civil war broke out between the English and the conquering Normans. The only legitimate son of Henry I had died and attempts to replace him with his daughter, Empress Matilda, started a power struggle between competing English barons and Welsh and Scottish invaders. After a carve up of various parts of England, unification and peace came about under Henry II.

Dunster Castle saw action during the English Civil War being held by both the Royalists and Parliamentarians but stayed in the same family until 1976 when Colonel Walter Luttrell gave Dunster Castle and most of its contents to the National Trust. Armed with this information I made my way up to the castle to meet Seamus Rogers, the General Manager of Dunster Castle and Gardens for the National Trust.

The National Trust is only the third owner of the property (things move slowly in Somerset) and property passed to it due to a combination of historic death duties and the sheer expense of keeping up such an historic building.

Seamus and I started talking about the building, but the conversation soon moved on to how people connect with their past and why people wanted to visit these iconic venues. In the past, the emphasis may have been on education with visitors being fed a diet of information and facts. Today, it is more about the 'experience' and enjoying oneself.

This change in attitude is also reflected in the current and future membership of the National Trust. Today, many members are middle aged, middle class and are possibly the last to have final salary pensions. Future generations are unlikely to have an extended retirement and will use Trust assets in a different way. Perhaps a whole generation will miss out and only grandparents and grandchildren will benefit from all these properties saved for the nation!

Ozy and I left Seamus and decided to walk around the perimeter of the castle, the grounds of which are free to enter. On the opposite side to the village is the Gallox Bridge, a packhorse bridge crossing the River Avill. It is likely that there was a previous bridge on the same site in the fourteenth century known as Doddebrigge. Ozy preferred not to use the bridge, but paddled back and forth in the shallow waters of the stream.

Just beyond the bridge is a working watermill which still stands on the site of the original mill mentioned in the Domesday Book. I usually buy my flour here, but on the basis that I was trying to lighten the load on my back, I passed by and made my way through the narrow streets back to the High Street.

The village still has a Medieval feel about it and once a year, in early December, they turn off all electric lights and illuminate the entire village by candlelight. A procession takes place with locals carrying lanterns followed by a rag-tag entourage of stiltwalkers, morris dancers, bell ringers and carol singers, together with the locals dressed in 'suitable' medieval costume. I was not quite sure what counted as 'suitable', but perhaps this referred to England's old sumptuary laws which dictated what various ranks or classes could, or could not, wear.

These laws went into some detail about what clothes and colours a king could wear (gold and purple silk), that wives of a yeoman may not wear any veil or kerchief made of silk, that no knight under the estate of a lord, esquire or gentleman, shall wear any shoes or boots having spikes or points which exceed the length of two inches (under the forfeiture of forty pence) and that everyone else had to dress like Baldrick and smell of dung.

On the way back to my starting point, Ozy and I took the path on our left just before the Visitors' Centre to visit the Conygar Tower. This was erected in 1775, although it served no practical purpose, save that it acts as a navigational aid and was a folly designed to enhance the landscape around the castle. The building is hollow and has no floors, nor ever had any. When it was built, it cost £76 11s 1/2d with £4 2s 6d paid in scrumpy for the workmen, and 'an entertainment' when it was finished cost £2 5s.

And after a climb up, the climb down and back to the coast.

A ROBINSON CRUSOE MOMENT

As the coast arched round, Ozy and I were the only individuals on the beach and I felt a little like Robinson Crusoe. It was only later that I found out that the writer, Daniel Defoe, had stayed in Minehead in 1722 and walked this very stretch of coast to Watchet.

There is something quite spiritual about walking along an empty beach with just the sound of the waves, sun glinting off the water and the worn out groynes, like rotten teeth, poking up from the sand. I was lost in my own thoughts when Blue Anchor came into sight, my lunchtime stop.

The area used to be known as Cleeve Bay but now takes its name from the pub built in the seventeenth century, The Blue Anchor. The pub is still there together with The Smugglers Inn set in the centre of the sea front and it was here that I planned to stop for my midday pint.

On occasion, research on an area turned up very little and Blue Anchor was one such place. There used to be a church there but, like a lot of things in Blue Anchor, it fell into the sea. This event was marked each year when a group of pilgrims would walk from Cleeve Abbey to see the site of their former church.

Whilst there must have been sufficient footfall to warrant building an inn there, the resort took off in the Victorian era when the railway came and the beach, with its gently shelving coastline, was perfect for bathing. In fact, Ozy in the spirt of his long dead ancestors, paddled in the gently lapping waves.

The painter, JMW Turner, came here in 1818 and painted the bay and cliffs in watercolours. The coloured alabaster found in the cliffs gave rise to the name of the pigment known as 'Watchet blue'. Apart from that, the village seems to have been bypassed by history, perhaps that was why it was so peaceful with only the occasional chuff-chuffing of the West Somerset Railway to break the serenity of the moment.

The Smugglers was quiet as well and I sat in its womb-like cellar bar drinking a pint of Cotleigh and chatting to the landlord, Keith. In fact, we chatted for quite a while (three hours) and by the time I left, and entered the bright sunlight of the day, I felt a little light-headed.

My Ordnance Survey map showed that I had to walk along the road briefly and I also noticed reference to a 'Black Monkey Lane' marked on my map to the south. Again, despite time on Google, I had no luck in finding out why this was so called.

I walked past the Blue Anchor, precariously perched on the cliff edge and deciding that another beer would not be advisable if I had to walk along the top of the cliff path.

The Ordnance Survey map accurately described the few miles between Blue Anchor and Watchet as 'mud and sand' and they were not wrong, although this mud and sand was a fossil hunter's paradise. It was also a good source of food for the lone egret I could see below me.

It was here that I managed to get lost. I had just dictated my audioblog as I walked and happened to mention that the waymarking was new and very clear. Unfortunately, it was clearly wrong and I ended up on the beach with a rapidly incoming tide. Swiftly retracing my steps, I headed back up to the caravan park from where I had descended and continued along the grassy field edge.

I made my way up to Daw's Castle, which I initially thought was a pill box, high above the town of Watchet. This castle has many names including Dart's and Dane's Castle but in its present form was named after Thomas Dawe who owned the land in 1537.

Originally Iron Age, the fort was strengthened by King Alfred to protect the coast from the Vikings in around 878. Again, it formed part of the Herepath. The Vikings did invade in 914, 987 and 997 with '*much evil wrought in burning and manslaughter*'. The castle even had its own mint, one of only a few recorded in Somerset, which produced coins from the reign of Ethelred II (978-1016) and thereafter five other kings. Coins minted here have been found as far away as Copenhagen and Stockholm.

Whilst the castle was the original site for the burh of Watchet, the population gravitated to the lower coastal area to the east and that was where I too was headed.

DIRECTIONS

MINEHEAD TO WATCHET

From the South West Coast Path statue walk along the seafront, passing by the West Somerset Railway station and the entrance to Butlins. At the end of the beach by the golf club, take a right and immediately turn left before the golf clubhouse to re-join the path to Dunster Beach, passing the beach chalets.

At the car park it is possible to divert to Dunster itself. Walk up Sea Lane, crossing the railway tracks and on reaching the houses look for the riverside trail. After passing the sheltered housing scheme, take the tunnel under the road and then head left up the steps and continue up to Dunster Village. Return the same way.

At the Avill Flood Relief Channel, turn right signposted 'Blue Anchor' and continue along the beach. Just past the large pill box at Blue Anchor, take the steps on the right to the road. Turn left (the WSR station is on the right) along the esplanade.

At the end of the esplanade, pass the Blue Anchor pub, taking care as initially no footpath. Turn left into the car park and right through a kissing gate onto a narrow track and then follow field boundaries and woodland paths. Just past Crow Covert and a campsite (see OS map) the fingerpost suggests a left hand turn to the left. IGNORE this and continue straight ahead into woodland, cross a concrete drive, re-enter woods before entering a caravan site. Continue to Daw's Castle. Exit by the remains of the castle, descend to the road and walk down the hill to Watchet, walking through the town to the harbour and the statue of the Ancient Mariner.

THE WATCHET ALE TASTER

I arrived in Watchet with plenty of time to spare before my next meetings – all of them in pubs! I therefore decided to walk around the town and explore.

At the first car park, leading onto the harbour, the local art group had painted a giant mural depicting the history of the town from prehistoric times, the invasions by Saxons, Danes and Vikings, the Domesday Book, boat building, Samuel Taylor Coleridge, the industrial age and coming of the railways, the odd pirate and an extra-terrestrial …

"An extra-terrestrial?" I hear you say. Yes, it appears that Watchet has a very similar rock and mineral formation to that of Mars, 140 million miles away.

For more information about the town, I had a look at the Watchet website and this describes itself as '*A charming little coastal town with an active marina, excellent holiday accommodation, an old port, quaint houses and shops.*' and this very much summed up the town which had a genteel feel about it; the sort of place where policemen still gave cheeky youths a clip round the ear and landlords asked if you wanted your pint in a jug.

Whilst I thought it quaint, others had grand ideas for the town and I had arranged to meet one of those visionaries the following day at the harbour. However, now I had an hour to kill before the pubs opened.

The first record of Watchet comes from the story of Saint Decuman who arrived in Watchet in the seventh century from Pembrokeshire in Wales. He left Wales to get away from 'worldly companions' (Somerset being an ideal place to do this) and sailed over the Bristol Channel on, either a raft or a cloak, in the company of his cow. Is this sounding awfully familiar? Remember Saint Dubricius who sailed over to England with his mate, Saint Culbone, on a cloak?

Once here, Decuman lived as a hermit, eking out a living from the produce of his cow and acted as a pastor and physician to the locals.

Veneration came after he was killed by a local pagan who cut off his head, which, as you will remember from Saint Beuno in Culbone, was an occupational hazard for any saint at the time. Similarly, Decuman picks up his head, blows on it and then pops it back on his shoulders – job done.

Watchet gets its name from 'Wacet', the blue dye found in the lias rocks from the cliffs. Supposedly, Charles I wore a coat of Watchet blue when he was beheaded on 30th January 1649. This jacket now resides at the Museum of London.

Throughout the next few centuries, Watchet thrived because of its port and proximity to the Brendon Hills that were full of iron ore, desired by the Welsh, across the water.

From 1564 the port was used to import salt and wine from France and then, after the harbour had been storm damaged and rebuilt, it was used to ship kelp (seaweed) in the early eighteenth century – the kelp was used in the glass making industry. However, it was the iron mines in the nineteenth century that made the town its money and I was going to find the remnants of the old railway line.

The West Somerset Mineral Railway, although now dismantled, had still left a legacy and I went off to find out where it ran from and to.

I wandered around the back streets of the town, past the closed pub, the Anchor, humorously owned by Mr Richard Booz (deceased) and soon came across the dismantled mineral line; a straight path, now used by cyclists and dog walkers. Tracing this back into the town I was able to appreciate its importance and the orientation board provided me with the information I required.

Iron ore was extracted from the hillsides in the Brendon Hills and, from there it was taken by boat to Newport and then to Ebbw Vale for smelting to extract the iron. In fact, it was the Ebbw Vale Iron Works that owned an interest in the Brendon iron ore deposits, but found it difficult to transport the ore, due to the lack of useable roads and the steepness of the terrain. So a railway was built.

The challenge for the railway was the incline with a gradient of one in four. This meant a great deal of earth needed to be moved and it took four years to build, becoming fully operational in 1861.

In addition to the iron ore, passengers were also taken along with coal, culm, lime, corn, flour, manure, building materials and 'other goods', according to an advert in the Somerset County Gazette. The first passengers were miners and their families who lived in remote Brendon villages and they were able to travel free of charge 'at their own risk', which suggests there was some danger, probably because the passengers travelled up the incline on 'makeshift boxes'.

The line had a short life however, due to cheaper imported ore, and by the 1880s, the mines went into severe decline and rail traffic all but ceased. In 1907 the Somerset Mineral Syndicate leased the railway and worked the mines again. But again, this was short lived with the line being used last to test and demonstrate an automatic signal warning device in 1911.

With the demise of the line on my mind, my next stop was The Bell to meet a local poet, author and Coleridge expert, Ian Enters. It was at the Bell that Coleridge started the Rime of the Ancient Mariner in 1797.

Today's Bell had a carpet and plush seats and a fine pint of ale. This would not have been the case two hundred years ago, when the pub would have been dark, smoke filled both from the fire and countless pipes of stinking tobacco and the ale, dark, chewy and sour.

As I placed my digital recorder on the table to take down Ian's words of wisdom, it struck us how easily we were able to record our conversation. In Coleridge's time, he would have carried a portable wooden writing desk, together with inkhorn, quills and dusting powder.

Ian described Watchet at the end of the eighteenth century as a working harbour; industrious, fishermen hauling their catches from their flat-bottomed boats, but also wild with the sound of the waves crashing against the harbour wall and the tidal flow rushing into the culverts and drains in the town. Added to this, the place had a palpable sense of history. Alfred had set up his burh on the hill above a thousand years earlier and Coleridge would have connected with that and have been in his element.

Coleridge would have spoken to the local sailors and fishermen, heard their stories and superstitions, many of which survive today. In the mist he would have seen ghost-like boats that looked as if they shouldn't be able to sail and these must have fired his imagination.

I had asked Ian if he was, perhaps, able to pen a few lines himself and, prefacing his reading by saying they were only scribbled notes, Ian read from his notebook:

I've been asked for a poem commemorating Coleridge drafting an early version of Ancient Mariner when at the Bell Inn in Watchet.

I've been invited to the pub for a drink, a conversation and maybe inspiration for my own poem in the bar of the Bell Inn in Watchet.
I've been thinking about the pub and the connections between creation, place and Coleridge as I peer in a half empty glass at home, away from the Bell Inn in Watchet.

And then:

Here in Watchet
Alfred at Daw's Castle
watches for invasion
from Saxon Court
and marshals his wyrd
for the Herepath march.
The Luttrells and Wyndhams feud
over narrow and standard lines.
Panniered donkeys plod up cliffs
to load lime-kilns with acid stone
while far below flatners skim
mud-flats to scour a catch
where mud-horses plough
beyond the end of the Mineral Line.

If only I could scribble so well!

I left Ian to his pint and staring into the fire to catch a quick biryani in Watchet's Indian restaurant ready for my next meeting with the local CAMRA group.

Watchet is unique in that it still retains the Court Leet system of medieval administration. This allowed the manorial court to exercise the 'view of frankpledge' (oath of fealty to a lord). Ancient posts in Watchet included the coveted position of 'Ale Taster' and I was about to meet a gang of them.

Watchet is rather a real ale Mecca with at least three award winning pubs and we were going to visit them all with Mick Cleveland, Richard Overall and Jules Pentland.

Our first stop was the Esplanade Club, opposite the harbour. This was built in the 1860s as a sail making factory and is now home to the boat owners club. This venue is perfect on a nice sunny day, sitting outside, glass of ale in hand, listening to the live music they often have playing. A perfect start to our Watchet pub crawl.

Next on the list was Pebbles Tavern. This place looked like it had been there forever although is just a few years old. If you like your pubs warm and womb-like this is the place to be. Ben, the landlord and owner, welcomed us and a more enthusiastic and genial host you would be hard to find.

Ben is passionate about local ales, ciders and now gins, of which he has countless behind the bar. From a standing start a couple of years ago, the tavern has won the Somerset CAMRA 'Cider Pub of the Year' and you can see why with forty or so of them stacked high on racking in the cool room. Drinkers wanting to try out a few are given a taster and after a few of these caution is thrown mostly to the wind.

Our little group stuck to beer, all except for Mick who had been warned off excessive consumption by his GP. Unfortunately, there was no Stowey Ale available, mainly my fault for not taking down a barrel the previous week as I had promised. However, the other beers on offer were perfectly acceptable alternatives and we were all soon glad that we didn't share the same doctor as Mick.

Our final port of call was the Star Inn, opposite Pebbles and here we had a nightcap or two of Betty Stogs from the St Austell Brewery. In Cornish folklore Betty Stogs was reputedly full-bodied, golden-hearted and just a little fruity and we were all feeling very similar after a testing night out in Watchet.

*****

On the basis of 'plures necat crapula quam gladius' - *the hangover kills more than the sword*, I would have to tread carefully along the cliff paths on the next stretch and Ozy was not keen to be on the other end of a lead lest I toppled over. However, help was at hand with a strong coffee in the offices of the Onion Collective, my first stop of the morning.

I was here to meet Georgie Grant, a director of the all-women group, who had set themselves up to take on tourism development projects in the town. I was also somewhat nervous as, the last time I had arranged to meet Georgie I was on my way to the AONB offices in the Quantocks and had fallen off my bike.

The Onions asked a very simple question to the townsfolk of Watchet, "what do you need for a stronger future?" The answer was to encourage more tourism into the town and so the group did just that; starting with the new visitor centre and boat museum.

The Watchet Boat Museum celebrates the history of 'flatner' boats local to this area. These vessels were used on the Bristol Channel, where the tides go out a great distance, exposing miles of mud flats. The boats were specially designed for the shallow waters and had a single sail and flat bottom with no keel to navigate the muddy waters. The fishermen would catch sprats, herring, shrimp, haddock and salmon often smoking the fish after returning to shore. The museum is housed in a former goods shed designed by Isambard Kingdom Brunel in 1862.

It may well have been these ethereal boats that Coleridge saw giving him the inspiration for the *Rime of the Ancient Mariner*.

With the boat museum now up and running the Onion Collective has moved on to an even grander project, 'The Work Foundry'. This is to be a quayside work-cum-living-cum-eating space with room for exhibitions, music and entertainment. Visitors will be able to stay in a number of self-catering 'pods' and experience all that Watchet has to offer which, from the enthusiasm of the team behind the project, will be fantastic.

Revitalised with coffee, I started my last day of Ozy's and my week-long trip.

We passed by the statue of a forlorn Ancient Mariner, albatross attached by a noose around his neck and the bronze figure of Yankee Jack, Watchet's famous sailor and singer of sea shanties.

John Short (aka Yankee Jack) was an able seaman and bosun on many a craft sailing out of the area and got his moniker after running the blockade in the American Civil War. But, it was his singing that brought him fame and, over the years, he memorized dozens of shanties including Rio Grande, Shenandoah, Blow the Man Down, A Roving and Spanish Ladies.

Jack was also the Town Crier, in charge of the local fire brigade and contributor to Cecil Sharp's collection of English folk songs in 1914.

HOMEWARD BOUND

This last part of the coastal path was, up until 2016, inaccessible due to lack of crossings across a number of inlets running out into the sea. Not only were there no crossings in some places, the tide levels also make the path impossible to navigate on occasion and one of these points was reached just out of Watchet at Helwell Bay. Prudently, I had downloaded the tide timetable and knew that I had plenty of time to cross the beach.

The rock strata here is stunning and some of the beach looked as if it were laid by hand. This stretch of the coast was also a fossil hunters' playground with ammonites in abundance. These fossils are the remains of a spiral-shelled sea creature that lived some 240 million years ago and named after the Greek ram-horned god, Ammon.

These creatures are the long extinct ancestors of our octopus, squid and cuttlefish and died out about the same time as the dinosaurs in the Cretaceous period. Whilst the fossils are prolific, this part of the coast was a Site of Special Scientific Interest (SSSI) and therefore hammering the fossils from the bedrock is forbidden.

This stretch of the walk is dominated by a plethora of holiday parks with their static caravans neatly laid out in rows. The park at Donniford was originally an army camp, again reminding me of the strategic importance of the Bristol Channel up until the Second World War.

At St Audries Bay I passed by the waterfall plummeting from the headland down to the sea and, for anyone keen on Channel 4's *Grand Designs*, this was where Kevin McCloud built his own hut and showered under the falls using soap he made himself.

Luckily, Ozy and I were spared the sight of a naked Kevin McCloud (or even the beautiful sea morgan reputed to be found at the base of the waterfall) and we continued along the beach looking for the opportunity to climb back onto the path above us.

To my right I caught a glimpse of Court House in East Quantoxhead. This was another Luttrell Family house, owned by them, on and off, since 1070. The present building was constructed in the latter part of the thirteenth century although the only part remaining of that period is the tower and the rest is seventeenth century and Jacobean.

Ozy and I then headed back down to sea level and a brief detour inland at Kilve.

Kilve is another fossil rich area and the beach today was strewn with the brightly coloured cagoules of a dozen or so school children, no doubt ruining millions of years of palaeontological history. This rock structure also hid another secret - Kilve crude.

Just inland from the beach is a building, looking like the funnel of an ocean-going liner, and this is all that is left of Somerset's fledgling oil industry. The plan was to build a shale oil extraction plant to pump out the crude, an eleven mile railway to connect Kilve with Bridgwater and an oil refinery at nearby Combwich.

The retort was built in 1924 by Dr Forbes-Leslie and its purpose was to distil the crude oil into useable fuel. However, the project never really got off the ground and never made any money. And I thought fracking was a new technology!

The road up from the retort led to the village of Kilve with its pub, The Hood Arms, and interesting tearooms, The Chantry.

This little church was constructed in 1329 for five monks whose job it was to say prayers for their benefactor, Simon de Furneaux. These chantries were built to facilitate the passage of the patron's soul though purgatory towards a speedy entry into heaven.

Perhaps, more usefully, the building was used frequently in the nineteenth century by local smugglers hiding their stash of brandy. It was probably this enterprise that finally did for the building when it burned down, possibly after the smugglers had to get rid of their contraband before the customs' officers came sniffing around.

Kilve has its very own dragon, Blue Ben, who used to bathe in the sea to cool himself after breathing fire on unsuspecting locals. Legend has it that Ben was caught by the devil who then rode him through the fires of hell. When Ben finally escaped he made the mistake of taking a short cut through the mudflats, got stuck and drowned. Ben's skull can still be seen at the Wells and Mendip Museum in Wells or the Museum of Somerset in Taunton (on rotation), Ben being an Ichthyosaur.

The large white building on the cliff-top is the Royal Navy aircraft range for RNAS Yeovilton and, up until 1995, this was used as a bombing range as well. This seemed somewhat dangerous to me although I presumed that any ordnance overshooting would only hit the south coast of Wales and the MOD were willing to accept this as collateral damage.

Ozy and I then stopped for a rest at Lilstock beach. There has been a habitation here since the Domesday Book and the name comes from the 'stoc' (farm) of Lylla and his people.

In Saxon times there was a port here and in the 1820s Sir John Acland built a boathouse on the beach with a pier and breakwater. Coal was imported for the nearby Acland estate and limekiln and the harbour was big enough to have its own coastguard and customs officer. There was even a plan to build a ship canal from Seaton in Devon to this point in 1888 but this never came to fruition.

In the 1860s and 70s the promenade became quite popular with pleasure steamers sailing between Lilstock, Burnham, Ilfracombe, and Cardiff. There was even a pub, the Limpet Shell, and this was in business at the beginning of the twentieth century, although derelict by 1932.

Sadly, the harbour fell into disrepair after a violent storm in 1900 and was never rebuilt.

I would have loved to continue along the coast, past Hinkley Point to visit the submerged forest dating back to 2500 B.C, however, it was here that I left the coast and headed inland.

The last of my villages en-route was Stogursey, just north of Nether Stowey.

The village's name comes from the manor of Stoke owned by the de Courcys – 'Stoke de Courcy', although there had been a settlement there for centuries beforehand and a hoard of Roman coins had been discovered in the area in 1999.

The village sits at the junction of two ancient routes. The first from the north coast and into the Quantocks, the other east-west from Combwich and along the coast to Watchet. It was the route from Combwich that would have been important to Coleridge as a ferry would have plied its trade from there to Pawlett Hams and this would have been the quickest route to north Somerset and Bristol.

Stogursey would have been an influential market town with its own market place at the crossing of the roads. It became a borough by 1225, and retained that status until at least 1833.

This was the final opportunity to sample a pint on route (and packet of crisps for Ozy) and we stopped at The Greyhound, the last remaining pub. In days gone by, my choice of pub would have been somewhat more extensive and in the latter half of the nineteenth century there were ten public houses in this small village.

We joined the locals at the bar, discussing the skittles and darts teams and, bizarrely, avian malaria in penguins. It seemed that the entire colony of Humboldt penguins had been wiped out at Exmoor Zoo recently. The zoo had named all of the penguins who had died, including; Buster, Newquay, Ludo, Percy, Lemmy, Truddle, Owlie, Blossom, Friendly and Arthur. Touching.

While we were in Stogursey I took the opportunity to visit St Andrew's Church. This was originally built by one of William the Conqueror's henchmen, William de Falaise at the end of the eleventh century. It was then given to Benedictines of Lonlay in north-western France (now Stogursey's twinned town). At some stage thereafter the church returned to the village.

The church has two fonts and an interesting iron ring known as the 'sanctuary ring'. This was used by those accused of a crime to seek sanctuary from the Church for a period of up to forty days. The system of sanctuary was complicated and often just postponed the inevitable, usually being strung up. In 1243 a murderer, John de Rechich, was granted sanctuary and then absconded before his trial. Where this occurs the church became liable for a fine. Finally, the church also houses an Ichthyosaur fossil found nearby – probably a relative of Blue Ben.

The route out of Stogursey took me past the original castle. This was similar to the motte and bailey castle at Nether Stowey, although this has a proper moat filled with water. It was the family home of the de Courcys, later owned by King John during the First Barons' War (the one that ended with the signing of the Magna Carta). During this time instructions were given to destroy the castle. However, luckily, this did not happen and the building is now a rather lovely holiday home.

And so the last mile of my journey took me back to Nether Stowey along what will be, in the future, the Two Castles Way (or something similar).

The Giants of Stowey would have travelled the route in a few strides. These were the legendary creatures who lived under the castle of Nether Stowey and regularly raided livestock and humans for food, foraging as far as Stogursey for their prey. However, Ozy and I were lucky enough to avoid the giants and soon found ourselves outside the Coleridge Cottage where it all began.

"One last pint?" I asked Ozy and he looked at me in that appealing, loving, Labrador way and so we popped in to the Ancient Mariner for a final real ale to toast Mr Coleridge.

"Thank you STC".

DIRECTIONS

WATCHET TO NETHER STOWEY

From the Ancient Mariner statue walk along the marina, cross the road towards the railway line, up the steps and turn left to follow the railway line. Pass the lookout post and then head down the steps to the beach. This part of the path is only accessible when the tide allows. Check the tide times at www.metoffice.gov.uk/public/weather/tide-times or call 03709 000 100 remembering to avoid high tide. On reaching a concrete single file slipway on the right, take this up to the lime kiln.

At the road, turn left past Donniford Farm and after 100 yards turn left to follow a concrete driveway to turn right just before the sewerage plant. Cross the bridge and at the road turn left and at the entrance to the holiday park, head right up a slope and follow the tarmacked track uphill. On reaching the field follow the left-hand field boundary. On nearing the end of the field, enter woodland on the left. Exit left onto a road and on reaching a car park turn left down a stone track. At the bottom turn right at the beach past the waterfall and use the two lots of steps to walk along the beach. IGNORE steps with a St Audries Bay sign and continue for 200 yards along the beach to take the steep grassy track on the right-hand side. Continue along the coast, following field boundaries until reaching Kilve.

At the grassy open area at Kilve, follow the tarmacked path inland to the oil retort and then turn left to rejoin the coast. At the Royal Navy range, pass by this to follow the coast (the path passes in front of the building but this is often overgrown). Head towards Lilstock Beach and just past the outfall sewer head inland and then branch left after 50 yards into the Lilstock Estate. Go through the side gate and head diagonally uphill keeping to the left field boundary. At the end of this large field, IGNORE the continuation of the coast path and head diagonally right to join a very straight hedged lane for a mile.

DIRECTIONS

WATCHET TO NETHER STOWEY CONTINUED

On reaching a road turn left and follow the road for half a mile and, just after a culvert marked by four reflective posts, it is possible to cut off the corner by walking diagonally across the fields. HOWEVER, this route is subject to potential diversions due to temporary field boundaries moving and unclear signposting. ALTERNATIVELY, continue along the road and turn right at the end towards Stogursey.

Whatever route taken, continue along the road to head towards a cream house and walk into Stogursey. At Lime Street it is possible to visit The Greyhound pub and further along the road is the church.

From the church, retrace your steps, turn left into Castle Street, heading towards the castle, round the moat to exit at the top of the leat. Continue ahead through four fields, keeping the field boundaries to the right. Keep walking in a similar direction through the next field (there may be a diversion) and pass to the right of a small copse of woods following the newly diverted route markers. Keep in a similar direction, keeping a field boundary to the right, walking gently uphill towards a gate. Again, continue to walk in a similar direction following markers where available. TAKE NOTE, this part of the path is subject to changes as it is soon to be a new waymarked path meaning the OS map is likely to be out of date. If you have a compass take the route in a SSW direction throughout.

The path will either end at the 30MPH sign on Stogursey Lane, in which case turn left into the village of Nether Stowey, or take you to the A39 where you should cross diagonally right to take a path between the village hall and Ancient Mariner pub.

For up to date directions please see:
www.coleridgewaywalk.co.uk/updates

MOGUL DIAMONDS

I said earlier on that the end of a long distance path can be depressing and ending this book could be equally so. However, I met so many interesting and helpful people during the walk; people filled with a love of the area and enthusiasm for what they did, that all of this rubbed off on me.

Coleridge was a prolific walker, and what I did as a one off, would have been "a walk down to the bus station" as Coleridge's great, great, great granddaughter, Rosemary Coleridge-Middleton, said at the opening of the sixteen mile extension, although I'm not sure there would have been buses at the time.

Rosemary went on to say that Samuel and his friends invented walking for pleasure and continued the activity when they all moved to the Lake District. Prior to that the only people to walk were the poor and destitute, vagrants and criminals. This is possibly why Coleridge and his friends were viewed with so much suspicion when in the area.

In Shondra Dell's book 'How to Start a Hobby in Nature Walking', she cites Wordsworth and Coleridge as early exponents of such leisure walking, identifying Wales and the Lakes as well as Germany and Switzerland as favourites.

The Victorians then honed the activity with the middle classes having more spare time and, to a certain extent, wanting to escape the inexorable progress of mechanisation and technology. They needed to get out of the cities, the smoke and the newly created stresses that modern life brought.

From the mid nineteenth century onwards walking clubs flourished until they found a communal voice in the Ramblers Association. The rest, as they say, is history.

The Quantocks and Exmoor may not have the grandeur of Scotland or the Lake District, or even the Brecons, lying to the north just across the Bristol Channel, but it does have the feel of being remote, yet never too far from civilisation. I met plenty of people along the path, whilst also spending hour after hour seeing no one. I never felt in the slightest bit worried about getting lost or being alone and spent many hours pondering life, the universe and everything.

I hope this book inspires you to follow in both my footsteps and those of STC and I leave you with this comment made by the great man himself on his lecture tour of 1811-12

ON READERS

Readers may be divided into four classes:
1. *Sponges, who absorb all that they read and return it in nearly the same state, only a little dirtied.*
2. *Sand-glasses, who retain nothing and are content to get through a book for the sake of getting through the time.*
3. *Strain-bags, who retain merely the dregs of what they read.*
4. *Mogul diamonds, equally rare and valuable, who profit by what they read, and enable others to profit by it also.*

May you all be mogul diamonds.

ACKNOWLEDGEMENTS

I would like to thank the following people for their help and support in writing this book:

Lynne Abbott, Glennys and Alan Pearson, Peter Barton, Charles Weeks, John Graham, Roger Kershaw, Chris McCooey and Angela Lees who proof read my manuscript and made helpful suggestions. Any mistakes are mine (please let me know).

All those at the Quantocks AONB and Exmoor National Park, in particular Chris Edwards, Iain Porter, Dan James and Georgie Grant (whom I was visiting when I broke my arm!).

Ian Faris (and the team at Coleridge Cottage), Greg Parsons at Cricketer Farm (thanks for the cheese), David Worthy, Colin Penny, Dave Harrison (and the Nether Stowey Facebook contributors), Rick and Teresa (Poole House), Revd. Val Plumb and the Stogumber Church Choir, Chris Jelley, Ian Cunneen (Mad Apple Cider), Yvonne Gay (Defining Moments), Seb Jay, Ian Mabbutt, Paul Marsh and Mitch (Miles), Jane and John Tucker, Ruth Hyatt, Dr Lita Strampp, Michael Hankin, Damon Wilcox (Encounter Walking Holidays), the team at Exmoor National Park Centre (Lynmouth), Cathy and Rod (Exmoor Owl and Hawk Centre), Dave Jackson (Beach Hotel), Paul Conibeare (West Somerset Railway), Seamus Rogers (Dunster Castle), Ian Enters and Mick Cleveland, Richard Overall and Jules Pentland (Somerset CAMRA).

Thank you to all those who fed and accommodated Ozy and me along the route and who enthused about the project:

Julian (Ancient Mariner), Bill (George Hotel), Charles (formerly of the Rose and Crown), Chris (Plough), Simon and Caroline (Notley Arms), Marion and Barry (Beechcroft), Mike (Valiant Soldier), Janet and Nigel (Myrtle Cottage), Simon (Staghunters), Debbie (Riverside Cottage), Ben (Pebbles Tavern) and Keith (Smugglers).

If I have missed anyone I'll put them into the next edition...

BIBLIOGRAPHY

Coleridge & Wordsworth, The Crucible of Friendship – Tom Mayberry
A Quantock Tragedy – David Worthy
The Old Quantocks, People & Places – David Worthy
Quantock Miscellany – Audrey Mead & David Worthy
Somerset Stories of the Supernatural – Roger Evans
Somerset Folk Tales – Sharon Jacksties
Thomas Poole & His Friends – Elizabeth Sandford
The Historic Landscape of the Quantock Hills – Hazel Riley
Samuel Taylor Coleridge – Seamus Perry
The Journey of the Louisa – Dee Jackson
How to Start a Hobby in Nature Walking – Shondra Dell

A great amount of research was undertaken on-line at sites too numerous to mention. Thanks to all those people who loaded up this information.

FOR FURTHER INFORMATION

Contact me (Ian):

01278 732228
info@theoldciderhouse.co.uk

The Coleridge Way Walk website contains up to date information on the path, photos of those walking, blogs, video and audio and updates on any route changes or amendments.

www.coleridgewaywalk.co.uk

Don't forget to follow us on Twitter @coleridgeway and use the hashtag #coleridgeway. Feel free to comment, make corrections, upload photos or inform me of any route changes or difficulties.